T0150407

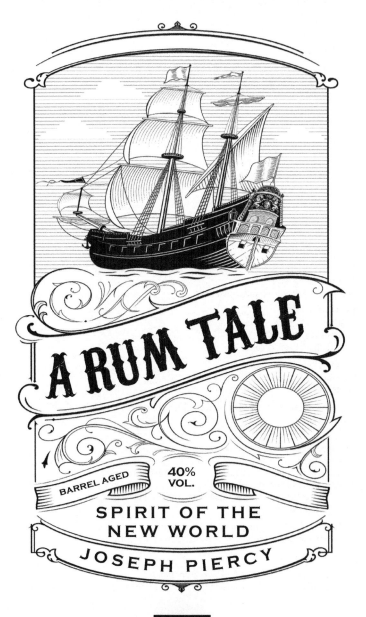

A RUM TALE

BARREL AGED   40% VOL.

SPIRIT OF THE NEW WORLD

JOSEPH PIERCY

The History Press

First published 2019
This paperback edition published 2020

The History Press
97 St George's Place,
Cheltenham, GL50 3QB
www.thehistorypress.co.uk

British Library Cataloguing in Publication Data.
A catalogue record for this book is available from the British Library.

ISBN 978 0 7509 9598 6

Typesetting and origination by The History Press
Printed and bound in Great Britain by TJ Books Limited, Padstow, Cornwall.

CONTENTS

INTRODUCTION

A RUM TALE

The story of rum is complex – as complex as the blending process involved in producing the best brands in the world's greatest spirit. It involves a cast of thousands to tell it anywhere near accurately. It includes some of the greatest heroes and villains of history: colonialism, pirates, wars, slavery and the growth of global capitalism. A ten-part, big-budget television series or a blockbuster Hollywood film would struggle to do the story justice. Key points, oddities and anomalies would be glossed over, ignored or conveniently forgotten. In short, it is an intricate, multifaceted story, which is by turns fascinating and absorbing, and at times downright alarming. This book tells only part of *A Rum Tale*.

The origins of rum are difficult to trace, but there is one indisputable fact: wherever in the world sugar cane is grown, rum (or something related to rum) is or has been produced.

The 'cast of thousands' I mentioned on the previous page include such historical luminaries as Christopher Columbus, George Washington, Admiral Lord Nelson, John Adams, Captain William Bligh, Ernest Hemmingway and, in contrast to his abstinence and brilliant exhortations that rum was 'a slave-owner's drink', Malcolm X – a whole host of major and minor characters throughout history who no doubt would have made for great dinner party guests, (whether rum was served or not). And yet rum remains, at least until recently, considered a 'childish' drink – something that neophyte girls order on a first date when their priapic beau takes them to a cocktail bar: 'Oh, I'll just have a Bacardi and coke please' – possibly one of the most revolting drinks in the history of trying to have something resembling fun.

Rum, however, is on the march. New small-batch distilleries are springing up all over the world, with new markets opening and 'rum festivals' becoming commonplace across the world. This both dark and light drink, steeped in history, is finally starting to find its place. I have to admit that this is probably because the sudden interest in gin from the mid 2000s has started to wane through saturation, so the thirst for the 'next big thing' has centred on rum. I like to think of rum as a sleeping giant in that context, unencumbered by market forces, a drink for those 'in the know', which brings me neatly on to the matter of tasting and evaluating rum. Unlike other spirits, rum has no international classification – basically anything goes. There are some fantastic and very learned 'rum scholars' writing books and blogs, of whom I am greatly indebted to researching and writing this book. Nonetheless I take issue with pretentious and meaningless tasting notes and refer you to David Hume (1711–1776); my book is for rum enthusiasts, that is people interested in the history of drinks they enjoy, not for elitist snobs. I hope it is a beginners' guide, so to speak, and doesn't smack of any snobbery or petty prejudice.

David Hume, the Scottish philosopher and historian, attempted to analyse the problem of how to define good from bad in matters of judgement and expertise in his essay 'Of the Standard of Taste' (1757). Hume was concerned with critical judgements and how (or why) one pronouncement can hold sway over another contrary point of view. One of the major concerns clouding critical judgements, such as claiming one rum was the best in its class over another, boiled down to an inability to distinguish between simple facts and expressions of sentiment and/or emotion. For example, an ardent supporter of a certain football team may witness a goal scored by their team that exhibits skill, balance and athleticism, and pronounce it a 'beautiful goal'. If the opposition, moments later, score a goal of comparable merit, it is unlikely to be viewed with dispassionate reason. This is because the initial judgement is coloured by sentiment and emotion, and therefore is subjected to prejudice. Critical verdicts based upon sentiment and emotion are devoid of any discernible truth value and thus rendered, in Hume's words, 'absurd and ridiculous'.

For Hume, standards of taste and their accompanying critical judgements are often determined by slight differences, nuances and subtle oppositions. As a general rule people respond to more obviously apparent aspects and qualities in 'things'. How many times have you heard people express pleasure at the sight of a sunset? Yet the sun sets every dusk all over the world, so why should one sunset be any more beautiful than another? This point, in turn, opens up questions about perception, time and place, or, if you like, 'being in the moment'. Some years ago, I visited filmmaker and wine producer Francis Ford Coppola's winery in Geyserville, California. It's a stunning estate, which contains a small museum of Coppola film artefacts and props. My wife and I toured the grounds and had a private tasting of the forty-plus wines they produce onsite (I hasten to add we didn't taste all forty wines but a selection of their vintages). If I am truly dispassionate in my assessment of the wines we sampled, they weren't actually that great, but there was something about sitting behind Don Corleone's (Marlon Brando's) desk from *The Godfather* sipping a fair-to-middling pinot noir that was very seductive on my judgement. I subsequently purchased a case of mixed wines to ship back home, but when opened and drunk back in the UK on a cold, wet November evening, they proved to be a profound disappointment. Situation, moment, sentiment, blimey, even the bloody weather can cloud judgements.

Hume makes this point about the 'fine margins of taste' and illustrates it with reference to Miguel de Cervantes' (1547–1616) timeless novel *Don Quixote* (1605). In one scene in Cervantes' episodic master work, Sancho Panza tells a story about two wine connoisseurs tasting and evaluating a barrel of wine, which they have been told is the finest produced in the whole of Spain. The first of the 'experts' samples the wine with the tip of his tongue, rolls it around his mouth, spits it out into a bucket and concurs that it is indeed of good quality and has a finish of rusty iron. The second 'expert' smells the wine, breathing deeply and agrees that it is of very high vintage but that the wine has a hint of burnt leather in its bouquet.

Some onlookers ridicule and dismiss the judgements of the so-called experts accusing them of making false and bogus judgements. However, when all of the wine has been drunk a rusting iron key and a burnt leather strap are found in the bottom of the empty barrel.

Hume deploys Cervantes' tale to illustrate his view that developing good taste is a matter of refinement that requires time and needs to be practised in as detached a manner as possible. For Hume, it is not a matter of determining if one stated position in contrast with another is true or false, or vice versa, but in deciding which is simply better according to certain principles. In summary, Hume sets out the following criteria for sound taste and judgement: 'strong sense, united to delicate sentiment, improved by practice, perfected by comparison, and cleared of all prejudice, can alone entitle critics to this valuable character of sound judgement and taste'. In other words, practice and perseverance, variation, considered comparison – find what you like and then measure according to that standard – and always looking for something new is what makes a rum connoisseur, not daft tasting notes about coconut husks and rotting mangoes.

I can't actually remember when I first tasted rum and thus if I actually liked it immediately. It is possible, even likely, that my first contact with the 'flavours' of rum wasn't through drinking at all but through cakes, ice cream and other sweet treats. This stands in stark comparison to other spirits. Experimenting with alcohol at teenage parties inevitably is a matter of trial and error, with more errors occurring to the novice drinker. I can remember being violently ill on gin – an experience that has coloured my ability to drink 'mother's ruin' to this day. Whisky too presented its pitfalls, particularly during my undergraduate years, and vodka only seemed to serve one notable purpose: to get drunk as quickly as possible (a position I later revised when I lived in Russia – although getting drunk in Russia is less of a vice than a necessity and national pastime).

I don't think I ever considered rum to be a childish drink, as was a common misconception in some quarters – quite the opposite, in fact. If I am to identify two people to thank for my love of rum, it is my father and his long-time friend Joseph Christopher (whom I am named after). My father met Joseph 'Joe' Christopher at Durham University in the early 1960s where they were both post-graduate researchers in the physics department. Joe Christopher was born and bred on the island of Bermuda, which has a rum-related history and culture thanks in the main to the Gosling Brothers (see Rums of Distinction: Gosling's Black Seal). My father didn't really drink alcohol (having come unstuck on Scotch at a student party) aside from the odd sociable pint of bitter in the Student's Union, or wine on special occasions. Joe Christopher introduced him to the wonders of rum, sales of which were in decline at the time with the market more or less dominated by brands such as Lamb's Navy Rum, Bacardi and, God forbid, Malibu (once considered the height of 1970s chic, which says it all really). It was rare to find any other varieties of rum in pubs and bars across the United Kingdom, let alone exotic marques from the Caribbean. My father and Joe Christopher (who returned to Bermuda on completion of his

PhD and eventually served as Minister for Education on the island) have remained firm friends for over fifty years and visited each other on numerous occasions. Whenever Joe comes to the UK he always presents my father with a bottle of rum, which is always of impeccable quality and taste: Appleton Estate's, Mount Gay's and, of course, Gosling's Black Seal, to name but a few. Whenever my family visit the Christopher family on Bermuda, it is tradition to bring back rum. It is for this reason that I have firm and fond memories of rum, of watching my father and his friend sitting, sipping together, reminiscing and laughing, often with an illicit Cuban cigar each to accompany the spirit, and listening to their tales and discussions long into the night. It is also therefore why I associate rum with being a sophisticated drink, drunk by men (and women – Joe's wife Marlene mixes a mean Dark 'n' Stormy) of stature and standing – a drink for grown-ups.

As mentioned previously, this book is an introduction to rum, the fascinating history behind the drink and a user-friendly guide to a marvellous spirit. Alongside the historical developments sit rum-related anecdotes and trivia, appraisals of some fine marques and brands, and some suggestions for cocktails. I have selected a baker's dozen of 'Rums of Distinction' but confess the choices I have made have been partly arbitrary and often determined by the back story to the brand and my own personal preferences. Rum is a truly global drink currently produced in over fifty countries across the world, and although Caribbean rums sit at the top of the tree and set a high standard, there are some fantastic rums being distilled, aged and blended in many other regions. With this in mind, I have tried to give an even spread when making my recommendations and apologise for any omissions that may offend. Considerations of time and space have also had a part to play.

Some books dedicated to a type of drink offer advice on how best to appreciate it, presenting a mannered approach – mix with this, don't mix with that, don't mix it with anything at all. Some rums lend themselves to certain mixers better than others (although arguably this is a matter of personal preference) while some are just so complex on the palate that to drink them sloshing in ice, with fruit juice or flavoured fizzy pop is borderline insulting. I have at points made suggestions for how I personally have best enjoyed a particular rum, but by all means experiment, explore and discover your own preferences.

If I have one major bugbear about modern cocktail establishments, however, it is the extraordinary amount of ice that bartenders use. This also enrages my father who spent an amount of time on a recent holiday to Barbados loudly admonishing bartenders for drowning his rum in too much ice. We have a 'one piece of ice' rule per 40/50ml glass when sipping a premium aged blend. This sets up a flavour journey as the ice slowly releases water, which in turn unleashes the aromatics. Any more than that and the drink becomes too watery too soon, washing away any subtle nuances.

Overproof rums need to be carefully watered. In fact, as a rule of thumb, overproofs, unless combined in a long cocktail, should always be watered and treated with respect – not to is literally to play with fire. Some years ago, my friend and rum connoisseur, Kal Elhasjoui, gave me a bottle of the now discontinued Ron Bacardi 151 overproof as a birthday present.

A disastrous and frankly bizarre evening ensued involving myself and Kal, Aubrey Smith, the illustrator of this book, and a minor 1980s indie rock star (whose name I shan't mention), which reached its zenith when my kitchen caught fire and almost burned down the house. Bacardi discontinued production and sale of Bacardi 151 amidst numerous legal battles with burns victims, so handle with care. You have been warned.

As I am writing this on an uncommonly warm February afternoon, the sunlight is streaming through the window and warming my face. Rum is a sun-drenched drink, redolent of Caribbean beaches and bars and fun times. Let's get started on our tour through the world of rum – a journey through histories and cultures which makes the story of rum so timeless. Enjoy!

Joseph Piercy
Brighton 2019

PART 1

A MURKY PAST

THE BIRTH OF THE SUGAR TRADE,
DISCOVERY OF THE NEW WORLD,
CHRISTOPHER COLUMBUS, THE SLAVE
TRADE AND ALL THAT ...

The beginning of the history of rum is inextricably linked to the history of sugar, or more precisely the cultivation of sugar cane. *Saccharum officinarum* (in Latin) is the most commonly grown variety of sugar cane, a fast-growing species of grass cultivated in more than ninety countries, with a worldwide harvest of 1.69 billion tonnes. The base material, however, had far more humble beginnings and took several millennia to spread across the world and become the biggest agricultural crop on the planet.

Botanists believe that sugar cane originated on New Guinea, a large south-western Pacific island with a unique climate and ecosystem perfectly suited for the grass to flourish and thrive. The first settlers on New Guinea are thought to have arrived some 50,000 years ago and were itinerate traveller tribes who made their way through the South–east Asian peninsula. Archaeological evidence found on New Guinea suggests these early inhabitants (from whom the various modern-day Papuan tribes are descended) developed sophisticated agricultural systems in the form of irrigation mechanisms and are thought to have practised crop rotation many centuries before their western counterparts.

In sugar cane they found an abundant source of calories, first chewing on the stems of the grass before developing other methods and tools to extract the sweet and sticky cane juice. Over time techniques of preserving the juice developed, largely to counteract the tendency for the extract to spoil quickly in the tropical climate – boiling the juice down produced a rich, honey-like syrup and heating the juice caused it to form into crystals.

The Papuans transported their crop first to Indonesia and the Philippines and eventually to mainland Asia, with sugar arriving in India and China around 1000 BC. The ancient Hindu texts that comprise the *Arthashastra* (a classical treatise on politics and economics written between the second century BC and third century AD) refer to a type of sugar wine (*gaudi*) and a spirit liquor thought to be a simple distillate of molasses known as *amlasidhu*. India embraced sugar, cultivated the growing of sugar cane and put the crop to a variety of uses. The grass was used as fodder for working elephants, sugar was used in medicine and religious rituals, and India also produced the first recorded confectionery bars – blocks of crystallised sugar syrup known as *khanda* (from which the modern word 'candy' derives).

Alexander the Great's (356–323 BC) celebrated general and explorer Nearchus (360–300 BC) visited India in 325 BC, sailing from the Indus river to the Persian Gulf and recording his expedition in his travel journal *Indica*. Nearchus was particularly taken with sugar cane, writing: 'In India there is a reed which brings forth honey without the help of bees from which an intoxicating drink is made.' However, despite Nearchus' recommendation, it was another 300 years before sugar appeared on the doorstep of Europe when it was exported to Persia from India in AD 600.

The establishment of the Umayyad Caliphate (AD 661–750) oversaw a rapid expansion of the Islamic world. At its height, the Umayyad's power spread from Pakistan to Portugal, conquering Egypt and most of North Africa along the way and constituting an empire of 4,300,000 square miles and 33 million people. The Umayyads were cultured and progressive both intellectually and socially. They established secular regulations that allowed Christians and Jews to practise their religions without sanction and side by side with Muslims. They set up democratically appointed advisory councils, minted their own currency and developed innovative technological advances in agriculture and water management. These latter developments led to the establishment of sugar-cane plantations in Egypt, Sicily, Malta, Cyprus and, by the eighth century, in southern Spain.

The achievements of the Umayyad were all the more remarkable given that the rapid expansion occurred within a matter of decades. However, not all factions of the Islamic world agreed with the Umayyad's progressive and liberal ideas, and the dynasty was overthrown by a civil war in AD 750. Whilst the majority of the Umayyad family were rounded up and executed, a few members escaped the purges and set up an emirate on the Iberian Peninsula in Córdoba, Spain, bringing to Southern Europe techniques for growing and refining sugar for the first time.

The demise of the Umayyad Caliphate did not diminish Islamic influence in the Mediterranean. By the middle of the eighth century Spain had fallen to the Moors who held sway in Iberia for several centuries, and several islands such as Crete and Malta became Arabic outposts during the ninth century. The Arabs and the Moors experimented with sugar-cane cultivation, borrowing ideas gleaned from India and Persia. The first industrial sugar mills, although little more than manually operated mechanical presses, were introduced from India to gain maximum yield of cane juice. Sugar was much in demand by Arabic physicians who experimented with the spice for medicinal purposes. It was in the area of agricultural production that the Arabs and the Moors excelled, and wherever they ventured they took their innovations with them.

The cultivation of sugar cane was a labour-intensive process with growing seasons of up to twelve months. As a subtropical crop, sugar cane required extensive watering, which tested the ingenuity of the Arab agriculturalists. The growing of sugar cane had stretched from Egypt and North Africa, across the Mediterranean basin and along the southern coast of Spain as far as Valencia. The Arabs, mindful of sudden seasonal shifts of climate and frosts in the crops grown further north, began to alter the traditional planting seasons so that the cane could be harvested in summer.

The southern sugar plantations had the opposite climate issue, particularly in Egypt and North Africa where rainfall could often be scarce in the summer months. Islamic engineers adopted and revised Persian irrigation and water transportation technologies such as the *noria* (bucket wheel) and built *qanats*, ingenious underground aqueducts that rely upon the power of gravity to feed irrigation systems. The remains of

the engineers' labours (*qanats* were built by teams of skilled labourers known as *muqannīs* – a lucrative and respectable profession) can still be seen to this day with *qanat* systems surviving in North Africa and Spain, most notably in Granada.

By the time Pope Urban II called for the First Crusade (1096–1099) to reclaim the Holy Lands from Muslim rule, Islamic influence had begun to wane across Southern Europe. Up to this point, Northern Europe had had little exposure to sugar and it was considered a scarce but valuable spice. The crusades were integral in introducing sugar in greater quantities to England and Northern Europeans. Albert of Aachen, the Frankish historian of the First Crusade, mentions discovering sugar in his twelve-volume *Historia Hierosolymitanae Expeditionis* (*History of the Expedition to Jerusalem*) written between 1125 and 1150):

> In the fields of the plains of Tripoli (Libya) can be found in abundance a honey reed which they call Zuchra; the people are accustomed to suck enthusiastically on these reeds, delighting themselves with their beneficial juices, and seem unable to sate themselves with this pleasure in spite of their sweetness. The plant is grown, presumably with great care and effort, by the inhabitants.

It was not long before the crusaders fell under the spell of sugar and alongside importing greater quantities they soon began supervising the cultivation and production of sugar in the conquered areas such as Jerusalem, Palestine and Jordan, where the sugar mill at Tawaheen es-Sukkar, near Jericho, was excavated in 2001. As more and more land was conquered or reclaimed from the Arabs and the Moors, more and more sugar plantations and production sites were garnered and requisitioned. This inevitably led to more bountiful supplies of sugar flooding into Northern Europe, although the fact that sugar was not as scarce as it had been previously did not radically affect the price. Sugar was seen as an artefact of wealth and status. In his book *Rum Revolution* (2017) Tristan Stephenson cites an annual audit from the Royal Household of Edward I from 1243 stating that the English Court purchased (and presumably consumed) 3,000kg of sugar at a cost of somewhere in the region of £100 per kg in contemporary money.

By the fifteenth century, Portugal had jumped on the sugarcane bandwagon and began explorations along the African coast. Central to Portuguese expansion was the nobleman Infante D. Henrique of Portugal, Duke of Viseu (1394–1460), better known as Prince Henry the Navigator. Gathering together a fleet of sailors and map-makers, Henry's primary intention was to find the sources of the West African gold trade established by the caravans that flowed into the Moorish city of Ceuta, a former staging outpost for the Umayyad Caliphate's conquest of the Iberian Peninsula.

Ceuta was captured in a daring raid led by Prince Henry's father, King John I (1357–1433), in 1415 and provided the Portuguese with a key strategic base to expand their empire and fend off the attentions of the Spanish Castilians with whom the Portuguese had a long-running feud. Emboldened by the success of the raid on Ceuta, Henry dispatched two sailors under his command, João Gonçalves Zarco and Tristão Vaz Teixeira, to further explore and map the West Africa coastline. In 1419 the two seafarers set sail in caravels, an innovative new style of ship developed from traditional Portuguese fishing boats. Caravels were smaller and lighter than standard ships used in the Mediterranean at the time, and their innovative design of lateen sails made them faster and able to sail 'closer to the wind'. Although the manoeuvrability of caravels enabled them to cover longer distances faster, the lightness of the ships left them at the mercy of volatile Atlantic weather patterns. Zarco and Teixeira's ships were blown badly off their intended course by strong Atlantic storms and drifted for several weeks before reaching land in the form of a small unmapped island they named Porto Santo (Holy Harbour). The sailors had unwittingly discovered the Madeira archipelago and, intrigued by the description of the islands' rich and fertile soil, Prince Henry ordered a second expedition to colonise the islands in 1421.

Initially the Portuguese colonists cleared areas of the dense laurel forest to grow grain, but the crop yields soon became economically unviable to export back to Europe. The settlers then took the bold decision to plant sugar-cane crops on Madeira – a step that was to form the beginnings of the colonial plantation systems later adopted in the New World. The subtropical climate and rich volcanic soil on Madeira provided the perfect conditions for cultivating sugar cane and, combined with Atlantic winds to drive the mills for processing, Madeira rapidly rose from a small colonial outpost to become the very centre of the European sugar trade. In 1444 the first shipment of African slaves arrived on the islands from Lagos to provide the cheap (and sadly expendable) workforce needed for the sugar-trade expansion, and within fifty years Madeira was producing and exporting 1,800 tons of sugar per annum: almost half the sugar consumed in Europe.

TIERRA! TIERRA! : COLUMBUS THE SWINDLER?

When lowly Spanish sailor Rodrigo de Triano took up his post on watch aboard the caravel *Pinta*, one of the support ships on Christopher Columbus' first voyage across the Atlantic, on the night of 12 October 1492, he can scarcely have imagined how unkindly history would treat him in the future. At around 2 a.m. a bleary eyed and no doubt exhausted Rodrigo spied something glimmering faintly on the horizon. Columbus' flotilla of three ships had been drifting since departing the Canary Islands five weeks earlier, supplies were running low, as was the morale of the crew, and Rodrigo could be forgiven for thinking his eyes were deceiving him. He watched the spot on the horizon for a few moments until he became convinced he wasn't imagining things before waking his crew with the famous cry: '*Tierra! Tierra!*' ('Land! Land!').

The captain of the *Pinta*, Martín Alonso Pinzón, verified the discovery and alerted Columbus (on the nearby *Santa Maria*) by firing a Lombard cannon, and the three ships set course for the island Columbus named *San Salvador* ('Holy Saviour') in the modern Bahamas. Rodrigo de Triano must have been ecstatic as they approached the island. He had, after all, just won the equivalent of the lottery.

The financiers of Columbus' expedition were King Ferdinand and Queen Isabella of Spain, and as an incentive to the crew (and deterrent against possible mutiny) they had offered an annual reward of 10,000 pieces of silver to the first person to spot land. However, when the expedition eventually returned to Spain the following spring, Columbus claimed it was he and not Rodrigo de Triano who first spotted land by citing a dubious entry he had made in his journal of the expedition dated the previous day where he describes seeing a light on the horizon like 'a small wax candle lifted up'. The Spanish monarchs accepted Columbus' claim and duly awarded him the prize, leaving the hapless Rodrigo de Triano, a broken and no doubt bitter man, to die in poverty and obscurity. There can be no way of proving the validity of Columbus' claim to the reward. The entry exists in his journal but could easily have been added at a later date and it certainly seems questionable why, having seen something unusual on the horizon, he chose not to investigate it, nor bring it to the attention of his crews.

Whilst the Portuguese interest in the sugar trade flourished, their nearest neighbour and rival Spain copied Portugal's example and set up sugar plantations in the Canary Islands (most notably Tenerife, Gran Canaria and Fuerteventura). Although the industrialised growth of sugar cultivation by the Spanish and Portuguese on these islands was based on the use of imported slave labour, one unusual and often overlooked aspect was that free workers in the form of Spanish and Portuguese immigrants settled on the islands and worked alongside the slaves. This was partly due to the need for sugar specialists to oversee and coordinate refining procedures and was also indicative of how European traders adopted a hands-on approach to sugar production.

Venice and Genoa flourished as the major centres of commerce in the Mediterranean as they engaged in lucrative trade with Egypt and Latin Syria to import eastern luxuries, including spices like pepper and cinnamon from East Asia and local products like silk, cotton, sugar and gold. The fall of Constantinople in 1453, however, had caused disruption to the traditional 'silk road' – the long-established land passage between Asia and Europe. The major European economic powers clamoured for safer and ideally faster and more efficient trading routes by sea.

The Italian astrologer Paolo dal Pozzo Toscanelli (1397–1482) proposed a radical solution to reaching the eastern Spice Islands by sailing west and sent a detailed map and plan to King Alfonzo V (1432–1481) of Portugal. The original letter and map have not survived, but a copy of Toscanelli's map and plans found their way into the possession of a young business agent from Genoa,

Christopher Columbus (1451–1506). It is known that Columbus' brother, Bartolomeo Columbus, studied cartography in Lisbon and it is possible that he passed the map to his ambitious sea-faring brother. Columbus was employed at the time as a business agent by wealthy Genoese families such as the Centuriones, for whom he made several trading excursions to Northern Europe in the 1470s. Portugal had close political and economic allegiances with Genoa, and Columbus based his operations in Lisbon between 1477 and 1485. Whilst residing in Lisbon, Columbus met and married Filipa Moniz Perestrelo, the daughter of Bartolomeu Perestrello, a Portuguese explorer and one of Henry the Navigator's captains who was the first governor of the recently established colony on Porto Santo where he administrated sugar plantations.

Columbus is likely to have visited the Canary Islands and Madeira on business and trading trips, and so had rudimentary knowledge of Atlantic navigation. In 1485, Columbus presented Toscanelli's plan for sailing 'west to go east' to King John II (1455–1495) of Portugal and requested royal patronage to fund an exploratory voyage. Much like his predecessor, Alfonzo V, King John and his advisors were unconvinced by Columbus' theory, believing quite correctly that Columbus had vastly underestimated the distances to travel in order to effectively circumnavigate the globe. Undeterred, Columbus resubmitted his plan to the king three years later, when it was again rejected. The explorer Bartolomeu Dias had returned from a voyage around the Cape of Good Hope (the first European to do so) and the Portuguese court were more inclined to explore further possibilities offered by this route to the east.

Columbus then spent the next two years lobbying the major courts and financiers of Europe to try to obtain financial backing for his expedition and sent a delegation to England to lobby King Henry VII but was turned down. Eventually, and seemingly on a whim, King Ferdinand (1452–1516) of Castile relented and overruled his wife, Queen Isabella (1451–1504), who had previously dismissed Columbus' project as far-fetched, and granted Columbus the backing and conditions he required.

Columbus initially set sail from Spain with a flotilla of three ships (a large carrack named *La Santa Maria* flanked by two smaller caravels *La Pinta* and *La Niña*) on 3 August 1492. The expedition stopped in the Canary Islands to pick up supplies and make repairs before setting out in open water on 6 September. Five weeks later, the three ships reached San Salvador in the modern-day Bahamas on 12 October (see *'Tierra! Tierra!'*: Columbus the Swindler?), although Columbus was convinced he'd reached the East Indies.

On San Salvador Columbus and his men were greeted by the indigenous Taíno people who were delighted to have visitors. Columbus described the inhabitants in his diary:

> They traded with us and gave us everything they had, with good will ... they took great delight in pleasing us ... They are very gentle and without knowledge of what is evil; nor do they murder or steal ... Your highness may believe that in all the world there can be no better people ... They love their neighbours as themselves, and they have the sweetest talk in the world, and are gentle and always laughing.

The Taíno presented Columbus with tributes of gold and pearls, and further travels to the islands of Cuba and Hispaniola (also known as Santo Domingo) unearthed hitherto non-European artefacts such as tobacco, turkeys, pineapples and hammocks, all of which Columbus presented to his delighted patrons at the Spanish Court on his return to Europe. In his diary Columbus notes that the Taíno would:

> make good and skilled servants, for they repeat very quickly whatever we say to them. I think they can very easily be made Christians, for they seem to have no religion. If it pleases our Lord, I will take six of them to Your Highnesses when I depart, in order that they may learn our language.

It is not known for certain if Columbus did actually kidnap any of the Taíno on his first voyage, but if he did, it is unlikely that any of them would have survived what proved to be an arduous and troubled journey back to Europe. However, judging by the evidence of his diary entry, it appears Columbus had ambitions to conquer and enslave the indigenous Taíno for economic gain and thus began colonial exploitation of the New World.

For his second voyage in 1493, Columbus commanded a vastly expanded fleet of seventeen ships, which transported 1,200 men plus equipment and supplies to set up colonies on the newly discovered islands. Columbus also transported 1,500 sugar-cane shoots, which many historical accounts claim were planted on the island of Hispaniola by Columbus' son Ferdinand, thus creating the first sugar-cane plantation in the Americas. The colonies certainly presented themselves as ideal for industrial-scale agricultural endeavours such as sugar-cane cultivation given the rich soil, plentiful water supplies and near-perfect climate. Columbus, as he had predicted, was easily able to subjugate the indigenous Taíno (and other tribes such as the Carib and Arawak) and put them to work as slave labour panning for gold and working on the plantations.

However, tragically, the peaceful and innocent Taíno were too gentle to survive the foreign invasion of their lands. The Spanish (and Columbus himself) conducted tyrannical atrocities on the indigenous people, who had no match for European weapons or war-mongering intent, violently slaughtering hundreds of the tribespeople at the first sign of dissent. However, the transportation of European diseases such as measles and smallpox proved to be the biggest catastrophe. It is estimated that within a single generation from Columbus' expedition in 1492 and the arrival on Hispaniola of the Dominican friar, historian and social reformer Pedro de Córdoba (1460–1522) in 1510, around 3 million Taíno had perished from disease and Spanish genocide.

The Birth of the Slave Trade

Columbus' and Spanish colonialists' early experiments with sugar plantations failed for a number of reasons. The rapid demise of the indigenous Taíno had largely robbed them of the workforce they required for the labour-intensive cultivation and refining of the crop. Although by the early 1500s the Spanish had begun to import African slaves to replace the indigenous workers, there was a serious skill shortage when it came to the knowledge and techniques required for large-scale production. The milling techniques the early *ingenios* (plantations) used were very basic and modelled on machinery used to press olives, which proved wasteful of resources and labour.

In 1515, a Spanish surgeon named Gonzalo de Vellosa set up plantations on the southern coast of Hispaniola. De Vellosa imported sugar experts from the Canary Islands who brought with them more advanced production techniques such as vertical rolling mills that could be powered by animals and water. Although de Vellosa's mills were initially successful (yielding an estimated 125 tons a year back to Europe), the Spanish Crown had a lust for gold and the patronage required to further expand and develop the sugar industry was sporadic and lukewarm. Increasingly Spain began to neglect its Caribbean interests in favour of searching for precious metals in Central and South America, leaving a vacuum that was later filled by British and Dutch incursions.

The Portuguese, meanwhile, who had been early adopters of sugar manufacturing on Madeira and Cape Verde, had found their way to mainland South America and established plantations on the Atlantic coast in the states of Bahia and Pernambuco (see Cachaça: When Rum Isn't Rum).

Initially the Portuguese used Brazilian natives as their workforce whom they captured on *bandeiras* – large-scale militarised slave-hunting missions. However, similar to the situation on Hispaniola, the captured slaves soon succumbed to European diseases, leaving the need to import the workforce from Africa.

BARTOLOMÉ DE LAS CASAS: 'PROTECTOR OF THE INDIANS'

Bartolomé de las Casas (1484–1566) was an early Christian missionary best known for his outspoken opposition to slavery and the atrocities committed by Spanish colonists against the indigenous people of the Americas. De las Casas was born in Seville and was the son of a local merchant who was one of the early Spanish settlers on the island of Hispaniola. Originally de las Casas was granted a plot of land on the island and granted a *hacienda* (business estate with a mine and/or plantation) and ownership of slaves. It is thought that de las Casas was initially ambivalent to the plight of the Taíno Indians and participated in slave-hunting expeditions. However, witnessing at first hand the atrocities committed and the wholesale deaths from disease, de las Casas turned to religion (he had no formal religious training) and was ordained as a priest.

In 1510, a group of Dominican friars arrived on Hispaniola led by Pedro de Córdoba. The remit of the friars' mission was to provide pastoral assistance to the colonists and convert the natives to Christianity. De Córdoba and his colleagues were so appalled at the treatment of the slaves and their suffering at the hands of their compatriots that they issued an edict withdrawing the right to confession for any of the island's slave owners, including de las Casas. Although no copy of the original edict has survived, de las Casas mentions in his historical writings that the friars' principal argument was that, so great were the sins of the slave owners, they were beyond absolution in the eyes of God, so why bother confessing anyhow?

Pedro de Córdoba had a profound influence on de las Casas, acting as mentor and confidant, and in 1515 de las Casas gave up his land and slaves and devoted the rest of his life to preaching against the evils of slavery. After returning to Spain to argue his case for abolition of the slave system, de Las Casas went back to the Americas as a missionary and was granted the administrative position of 'Protector of the Indians' – an advocacy and advisory position on slave rights.

In 1542 de Las Casas wrote his most famous work, *A Short Account of the Destruction of the Indies* – a diary of his experiences as a missionary and treatise against slavery. The manuscript was sent to King Charles V and is thought to have influenced the Holy Roman Emperor to issue the New Laws (1542), which restricted the use of indigenous tribes as slave labour.

Portugal had been the first European country to import African slaves as early as the 1440s and their strategic trading posts on Africa's Gold Coast ensured a plentiful supply. The Portuguese developed what became known as 'the middle passage' – a triangular trade route that linked Africa, Europe and the New World – and the first successful voyages of slave transportation were completed around 1510. The establishment of the middle passage was a key development of the Atlantic slave trade, with other European countries soon following Portugal's lead. The importing of African slaves also enabled Portugal to establish herself as the major producer and importer of sugar – a position of dominance that lasted for a century.

In 1630, Hendrick Corneliszoon Lonck (1568–1634), a Dutch sea admiral, led a successful raid on the Portuguese colonies in Brazil. Lonck commanded a flotilla of fifty-two warships and sloops, and a private army of some 4,000 men, bankrolled by the recently established Dutch West India Company. The raid proved successful, capturing the city of Olinda and the strategic port of Recife, and forcing the Portuguese governor and grandson of Duarte Coelho (see Cachaça: When Rum Isn't Rum), Matias de Albuquerque (1580–1647), to surrender control of the Pernambuco province. Although Albuquerque's resistance was short-lived in the battle with the Dutch, it is interesting to note that prior to retreating from the port of Recife, he ordered all of the sugar warehouses to be burned to stop the Dutch from commandeering them and benefitting from the profits they generated. The main objective of Lonck's raid was for his paymasters, the Dutch West India Company, to gain a foothold in the increasingly valuable sugar trade. Accordingly, the Dutch began to set up further plantations along the Atlantic coast of Brazil.

The Dutch conquest of Pernambuco was relatively short-lived, lasting barely two decades with the Portuguese finally reclaiming their colonies by the mid 1650s. Having lost their foothold in Brazil, the Dutch West India Company turned their attention to the Caribbean islands that had been sur-reptitiously claimed by the British and the French. The Dutch West India Company, having had their fingers burned fighting the Portuguese for a quarter of a century, had little appetite to pick a fight with their Northern European neighbours but saw an opportunity to protect their commercial interests in the area by providing trade and export routes for commodities such as sugar, cotton, tobacco and eventually rum.

Sugar cane was introduced to Barbados in 1640 and transported from the then Dutch-controlled Pernambuco. Initially, the Dutch traders provided financing and supplied equipment and African slaves, and transported most of the sugar to Europe. However, the political turmoil of the English Civil War made the fragile trade arrangements with the Dutch uneasy. The sugar industry had completely transformed the economy of Barbados, which up until that point had concentrated largely on a small and not very successful cultivation of tobacco. Tensions had been rising over the mercantile activities of the Dutch, with the British Parliament disturbed that Barbados was trading freely with the Netherlands. The governor of Barbados, Lord Willoughby (1614–1666), was an avowed Royalist and outspoken opponent of Oliver Cromwell who had sought sanctuary in Holland before emigrating to

Barbados where he had been appointed governor by the exiled Charles II. The Commonwealth Parliament passed various acts to enforce trade embargoes between British and Dutch merchants and Barbados in an attempt to bring the colony into line – all of which Willoughby more or less ignored. Eventually, Parliament lost patience and sent seven warships to the Caribbean to take control of the island and arrest the Royalists.

Despite these upheavals, the influence of Dutch merchants on the development of the sugar trade, and by extension the development of rum, cannot be underestimated. Indeed, some sources state that it was a Dutchman, Pietr Blower (dates unknown), who set up the first distillery on Barbados in the 1630s, thereby creating one of the key characteristics of Caribbean commerce and culture.

PART 2

THE RISE OF RUM

Sugar and Spice and all Things Nice and the Real Pirates of the Caribbean

Exactly where and when the sugar-cane-based spirit we know generically as rum was first distilled in the Caribbean is a matter of conjecture and to some degree controversy. The claims of certain modern producers regarding their history and heritage are often dubious at best, leading to an ongoing historical debate full of conflicting theories and arguments. The Moors, along with many other examples of culture and technology, introduced distillation techniques to Europe as early as the eleventh century. By the latter half of the fifteenth century early forms of whisky were being produced in Scotland and Ireland. This early whisky or *aqua vitae* ('water of life') was initially produced in monasteries for medicinal purposes such as the treatment of smallpox and colic. Rum, or at least a cane-spirit ancestor related to modern rum, was a slow burner both in terms of timescale and taste.

As noted earlier, Nearchus wrote of sugar being used in India to produce an 'intoxicating drink' as early as the third century BC, although there is no evidence of distillation practices and so this was more than likely a primitive form of sugar wine.

As sugar-cane plantations spread across most of the Caribbean in the mid-seventeenth century, early settlers had to content themselves with a variety of other forms of homemade hooch. The English colonist Richard Ligon (1585–1662), fleeing the turmoil of the English Civil War, emigrated to Barbados in 1647 where he promptly purchased a sugar plantation. Ligon recorded his experiences of life on Barbados in his book *A True and Exact History of the Island of Barbadoes* (1657) and describes the native inhabitants drinking a form of spicy potato beer made with ginger, sweet potatoes and root ginger. Ligon was also taken with another locally made drink known as *ouicou* in the language of the Carib Indians. Ligon describes how Carib women produced the drink by chewing cassava in their mouths then spitting the resulting mush into containers filled with water and mashed cassava, and leaving the pots out in the sun to ferment. The saliva from the women provided the enzymes to convert the starchy cassava roots into sugars that then fermented in the heat, aided by drifting yeast spores from other crops. Due to the scarcity of certain common European luxuries in the New World, the colonists experimented with producing wines from the locally growing fruits and crops. Pineapple wine was a particular favourite with Ligon who noted in his book that it was so delicious, it must be 'the nectar that the God's drunk'.

One of the major logistical issues facing the sugar-cane industry had been the extraordinary amount of waste left over after the refining process. The yield of valuable and sought-after sugar crystals left behind a thick syrupy sludge of molasses, which nobody had found an effective way to utilise. The colonists had tried various options such as using it as animal feed or crop fertilizer with limited results. Mostly it is thought that the molasses was given to the slaves on the plantation to do with as they wished. The sickly sweet syrup could be mixed with grains and other spices and left out in the sun to bake a form of sweet bread, or more pertinently left to ferment into a form of molasses wine, known in Spanish as *guarapo*.

One issue with *guarapo* (a form of which exists today in Cuba and Colombia where it has evolved into a sort of sugar-cane smoothie) was that it could not be preserved or stored for any notable length of time. Richard Ligon mentions a drink 'made from the skimmings of the coppers, that boil the sugar, which they call Kill Devil'. It is thought the 'coppers' Ligon mentions were copper stills and 'Kill Devil' a distillate of molasses. However, when listing the most common drinks on the island, Ligon places kill devil fairly low, suggesting that although a form of rum was produced in the mid-seventeenth century on Barbados, it took time to take off.

The origins of the name kill devil are unclear. It is possible that the fiery taste gave rise to a colloquialism that the drink was hot enough to literally kill the devil. Etymologists have presented various arguments regarding kill devil being an anglicisation of the original French word for fermentation, *guiller*, which lent itself to the French word for the drink produced in the Caribbean, *guildive*. However, it is thought that the French colonies set up distilleries on their islands after the British and so any passing phonetic similarity may be entirely coincidental.

Quite how or when kill devil morphed into rum is also hard to pinpoint. It is often stated that rum is an abbreviation of the word 'rumbullion' – a word of Devonian origin that may have been imported to Barbados by West Country settlers. Given that Bristol was the principal port trading with the Caribbean at the time, this is a plausible explanation, although some commentators have suggested that rumbullion originally referred to a 'tumultuous uproar' such as a riot or uprising. The earliest citation for rumbullion as a drink can be found in a document housed in the archives of Trinity College, Dublin. The pamphlet titled *A Briefe Description of the Island of Barbados* (circa 1651), thought to be the work of

CACHAÇA: WHEN RUM ISN'T RUM

Brazilians are extremely proud of their de facto 'national drink' cachaça but get extremely irate if anyone calls it 'Brazilian rum'. It is likely that they have good reason to feel aggrieved, as historical sources suggest that cachaça predates rum, certainly in terms of industrial production, by at least a century, lending credence to the Brazilian argument that rum developed from cachaça and not, as is commonly assumed, vice versa.

In 1535 the Portuguese nobleman and military commander Duarte Coelho Periera (circa 1485–1554) arrived in Brazil with a band of colonists. Duarte Coelho had participated in various expeditions to the Orient and had a successful military career as a commander in the Portuguese Navy. As reward for his good service, King Dom João III appointed Coelho as the governor of the Pernambuco captaincy – a region along the Atlantic coastline. Coelho's original remit had been to 'police' the area from frequent incursions from the French who were 'illegally' pillaging valuable Brazil wood. Coelho, however, had other ideas. Having served as a soldier on the Atlantic islands of Madeira and São Tomé, he was acutely aware of the potentially lucrative profits from sugar-cane cultivation.

Coelho founded the settlement of Olinda and set about enthusiastically planting sugar cane. Pernambuco – with its warm, even climate, without great variations in temperature and with regular rain – was a perfect location for the cultivation of sugar cane. Although not particularly liberal by contemporary standards, Coelho adopted a progressive approach to his colonisation project. He attempted to keep peace with the local Tupi Indian tribes, going as far as encouraging his brother-in-law to marry the daughter of a chieftain of the Tabaraja (a particularly belligerent, war-like tribe). Coelho had enlisted the help of sugar masters from Madeira who brought with them know-how and the most up-to-date developments in sugar production, including copper stills for distilling leftover cane juice. The resulting drink, named *aguardiente de cana* ('cane fire water') quickly became very popular, particularly with the native Indians – so much so that Coelho paid his workers in residual cane juice for them to distil – and cachaça as it is known today was born.

The sugar plantations in Pernambuco flourished under Coelho's governorship and guidance. He encouraged the population to plant sugar cane by offering the incentive of tax exemptions for setting up factories and the rights to export sugar. He supervised the construction of dockyards to build ships to export the sugar back to Europe and started using stocks of cachaça as a bargaining product with African slave traders, who had rapidly developed a taste for the 'fire water'.

Cachaça has been developed and refined over the centuries and remains extremely popular in Brazil, where around 1.5 billion litres are produced per year, mostly for the domestic market, by over 40,000 registered producers. The drink is best known outside of South America as the mainstay of certain tropical cocktails, most notably as the base of the classic caipirinha. Although only around 1 per cent of the annual production is exported, interest in cachaça has grown in recent decades, with small artisan producers springing up and developing 'aged' and spiced varieties such as the Bartolomeu brand, named in honour of Bartolomeu Dias, the Portuguese navigator who was the first person to sail around the Cape of Good Hope. However, the lingering resentment from Brazilians towards the global reception of their favourite drink still remains. A 2013 trade agreement between the United States and Brazil contained a clause insisting that the words 'Brazilian rum' be outlawed from any product descriptions of cachaça exported to the USA.

Giles Silvestor, a sugar-plantation owner, states: 'the chief fudling [sic] they make in the Island is *Rumbullion*, alias *Kill-Divil* [sic], and this is made of sugar-canes distilled, a hot, hellish, and terrible liquor.'

To confuse matters further, other origins for the word rumbullion have been put forward including that it could have derived from shortening the Latin word for sugar (*saccha*rum), or the Romani word *rum* meaning powerful and potent, or the Sanskrit word for water (*roma*). A simpler theory is that the word 'rum', a colloquial term in Elizabethan times for something excellent, was combined with the French word for hot liquid, *buillon*, thereby giving us a description of a fine, hot drink – although Giles Silvestor was clearly not a fan.

Although historians and etymologists continue to scratch their heads about the origins of the name, by the latter half of the seventeenth century the word rum had become the dominant term for sugar-cane spirits. English explorer and historian George Warren (dates unknown) published a pamphlet in 1667 titled 'An impartial description of Surinam upon the continent of Guiana in America', which stated that 'Rum is a spirit extracted from the juice ... called Kill-Devil in New England'. Rum to the English, *ron* to the Spanish, *rhum* to the French – let us keep things simple from now on.

The expansion of the sugar plantations across the Caribbean continued to flourish, reaching St Kitts, Antigua, Montserrat and Guyana, with distilleries springing up alongside the sugar mills. The exportation of rum to Britain and Europe took some time to gather pace with only a miserly 22 gallons reaching the port of Bristol in 1697.

The reasons for rum's initial snail-like development as an important commodity are twofold. Firstly, the social structure of Barbados had quickly established along the lines of the Northern European model. A landed gentry of plantation owners sat at the top of the pile looking down on a white working class of indentured volunteers, who in turn held sway over deported convicts and undesirables (see Barbadosed) and the hapless slaves (indigenous and imported). Rum was most certainly produced but had the reputation of being a 'slave drink' among the higher echelons of the new Bajan hierarchy. Secondly, the quality of the rum being produced at this time resembled little more than a form of fiery moonshine made by distilling the skimmings or scum from the sugar refineries.

The desire to maximise profits from sugar production led plantation owners to produce a higher-quality dark muscovado sugar and then re-boil the waste to produce a lower-quality sweetener known as *peneles*. This had the advantage of minimising waste with any molasses, as noted above, used for other domestic purposes. However, it also put a limit on the quantity of rum produced. A form of semi-refined sugar was much in demand in Europe with a value of roughly double the price of muscovado, but its production invariably meant greater waste. It became a matter of simple economics: produce the higher-value sugar but find a way to utilise the waste (molasses). This was the point when rum really began to take off as distilleries switched from using the scum to distilling the molasses.

The early Caribbean distilleries were fairly basic, containing mostly a single pot connected to a condenser.

Richard Ligon describes a distillery on Barbados that contained a two-pot system connected to a cistern, which may have been based on techniques for producing malt whisky in Scotland. The fledgling rum makers experimented also with recipes, adding and combining different elements of the distillation process, which led not only to rum being produced in greater quantities but to a spirit of considerably higher quality.

Jamaica Enters the Sugar Game

Christopher Columbus claimed Jamaica for the Spanish Crown on his second transatlantic voyage in 1494, naming the newly acquired island Santiago. Although Columbus inadvertently returned to Jamaica on his fourth and last voyage in 1503 (see Columbus and the Night of the Blood Moon), a Spanish colony wasn't officially created on the island until 1509 under the proto-governorship of Columbus' son Diego.

The island that the Taíno natives referred to as Xaymaca (which gradually became Jamaica) was held by the Spanish for nearly 150 years but was used mostly as tobacco plantation with only small crops of sugar cane being grown, mostly for local consumption. The Spanish obsession with searching for gold in Central and South America left Jamaica badly neglected in terms of protecting itself and it was frequently attacked by English and French privateers (a polite term for pirates – see The Real Pirates of the Caribbean).

In 1655, under orders from Oliver Cromwell, Vice Admiral William Penn set sail from Barbados with a fleet of

BARBADOSED

The term 'barbadosed' refers to the practice, initially adopted by Oliver Cromwell following the English Civil War, of rounding up Irish men, women and children who refused to vacate their land and transporting them to the colonies (mainly Barbados) to work as slaves on plantations. These people worked alongside, and under the same conditions as, black slaves, and were subjected to the same inhumane treatment.

Not being satisfied with working these people into the ground, the plantation owners also bred barbadosed Irish women with black male slaves in order to produce the 'mulatto', a more valuable form of house servant.

In the early years of the colony's growth these two groups, both suffering the same harsh conditions, joined forces to organise regular uprisings against the English settlers, often taking advantage of raids by Spanish and French pirates to coincide with their revolts.

As the production of sugar cane increased, so did the need for labour to harvest it, and the population of slaves on the island increased from 5,680 in 1645 to over 40,000 by 1667. In order to increase their labour stocks, it became necessary for the criteria for barbadosing to become broader: convicted criminals were included, followed by the kidnapping of vulnerable people who were unable to defend themselves. Thousands of teenagers and children, along with prostitutes, were rounded up and shipped off to Barbados as the demand for sugar cane grew. William of Orange (William III) continued Cromwell's practice of barbadosing Irish political prisoners during his reign (1689–1702) and, later, George II extended it to include Jacobite rebels rounded up after the battle of Culloden in 1745.

Alongside those who had been forcibly transported to Barbados were a group of workers who were termed 'indentured labour'. These people voluntarily signed up for a set period of time, often five years, to be employed as paid servants on the plantations. This brought about a class system of its own on the island: landowners, servants and slaves.

By the 1880s, when a census was conducted (after the emancipation of African slaves in 1834), none of the inhabitants were identified as being Irish. There was, however, a small pocket of poor whites, named locally as 'redlegs', who may have been the descendants of the original barbodosed Irish.

thirty-seven warships and thousands of troops with the intention of plundering the Spanish island of Hispaniola (no doubt with an eye on the sugar plantations). Penn's plan of attack was poorly executed, however, with the British encountering heavy losses, and they were easily held at bay by the Spanish whom (unbeknown to Penn) had recently reinforced their military presence on Hispaniola.

Mindful that Cromwell would not look kindly on his botched campaign, and not wishing to return home empty handed, Penn directed his remaining ships north to Jamaica.

This time Penn and his men were successful, not through any particular military strategy but simply by force of numbers (Penn commanded an army of 6,000 albeit weary troops and the entire population of Jamaica at the time is estimated at no more than 2,500). Although the Spanish attempted to reclaim the island several times in the following years, the British governor employed the use of buccaneers (another polite term for pirates) and privateers alongside a small fleet of English warships to protect the colony. A good deal of political capital was garnered from the successful defence of the island but, in truth, Spain's heart wasn't really in it as the bottom had pretty much fallen out of the tobacco market and so they (mistakenly) viewed the island as of little commercial value.

The burgeoning riches and the developing success of Barbados encouraged the British settlers to all but abandon growing tobacco in favour of planting sugar cane (and later coffee and cocoa). It remains a curious oversight of Spanish imperialism that they failed to notice Jamaica had ideal conditions for growing cane, and within a century Jamaica rivalled and eventually superseded Barbados at the top of the Caribbean sugar tree. Inevitably, where there is sugar grown there is rum produced, and a fierce rivalry exists to this day between the rum producers of Jamaica and Barbados.

The Real Pirates of the Caribbean: Sir Henry Morgan

There is some dispute amongst rum scholars as to the role pirates played in the history and early development of the spirit. Whilst it is certainly true that the swashbuckling, free-wheeling, loveable rogues of literature and film, such as Long John Silver of Robert Louis Stephenson's *Treasure Island* (1883) and Captain Jack Sparrow of Disney's *Pirates of the Caribbean* film franchise, belong more to the world of fiction than fact, pirates had an important role to play in the early years of the fledgling colonies in the Americas.

The use of privateers, essentially soldiers of fortune, was key in defending different countries' interests. The line between what separated pirates from privateers and buccaneers was frequently blurred, although a strict definition exists in 'legal' terms (see Pirate Buccaneer/Privateer). Perhaps the most famous British 'pirate', Sir Henry 'Captain' Morgan (1635–1688) was originally a British soldier and then a privateer before arguably turning to piracy. Morgan's exploits in the Caribbean in the mid-seventeenth century have become folklore and are the inspiration for countless works of fiction, most of which are pirate related, and, of course, his name is attached to one of the major rum brands in the world – Captain Morgan.

COLUMBUS AND THE NIGHT OF THE BLOOD MOON

On 25 June 1503, Christopher Columbus landed inadvertently on Jamaica after being blown off course by a tropical storm. Columbus had been sailing around the Caribbean for almost a year. His ships were battered and damaged, and his crew was exhausted and riddled with diseases. Inspections of his two remaining ships confirmed the navigator's fears: they were no longer fit for purpose, and he and his men were effectively shipwrecked.

At first Columbus' men were able to trade goods with the kindly Taíno who provided them with food, water and shelter in return for the usual trinkets and chattels. After several months, however, the relationship with the indigenous population began to sour, no doubt due to Spanish sailors exploiting Taíno women amongst other atrocities, and the Taíno chiefs withheld their support for the stranded seamen.

Columbus dispatched a small crew of his men, accompanied by Taíno guides, to paddle in canoes to the Spanish colony of Hispaniola to raise a rescue mission. The mission was a daring endeavour, entailing paddling some 250 nautical miles across volatile seas, and took an estimated six days to complete. However, the pleas for a rescue mission from Hispaniola were rejected at first by the governor, Nicolás de Ovando y Cáceres (1460–1511), principally because he despised Columbus.

Meanwhile, Columbus and his men were starving, and in desperation (or so legend has it – we only have Columbus' word for it) the famous navigator hit upon a cunning plan. After consulting his nautical and astronomical charts, Columbus discovered that a lunar eclipse was due on 29 February 1504. On the day in question, Columbus gathered together the tribal chieftains of the Taíno and told them that God (Christian God) was displeased with them withdrawing their hospitality and that he would send a sign that evening by turning the moon the colour of blood.

The Taíno weren't convinced so Columbus told them he would retire to his quarters and pray to God for mercy and their salvation. Columbus (at least according to his albeit one-sided account) timed his stunt to perfection and when he emerged, once the eclipse had passed, the terrified Taíno threw themselves at his feet and showered him and his men with food and nourishments. Eventually the canoeists on Hispaniola were able to persuade Nicolás de Ovando y Cáceres to change his mind and a small flotilla of caravels was sent to Jamaica to ferry Columbus and his surviving men off the island.

Henry Morgan was born in Llanrumney, Wales, on 24 January 1635 and is thought to have been the son of a local farmer and landowner, Robert Morgan. Details of Henry's early life remain sketchy although it is probable he either signed up or was conscripted into the military rather than pursuing a life in agriculture. Morgan arrived in Jamaica in the mid 1650s and again there is some dispute as to how or why. The most commonly held view is that Morgan was part of Cromwell's army sent to attack Spanish interests in the Caribbean in 1654, and under the guidance of Vice Admiral William Penn took part in the successful capture of Jamaica in 1655. An alternative view is presented by the French–Dutch writer Alexandre Olivier Exquemelin, a former surgeon who served under Morgan in the 1670s. Exquemelin's work *History of the Buccaneers of America* (1678) states that Morgan was kidnapped in Bristol and shipped to the Caribbean as an indentured white servant (see Barbadosed) – a fact hotly disputed by Morgan (see First-Hand Account or Fake News?).

By the early 1660s, however, Morgan is thought to have joined with a group of privateers led by Sir Christopher Myngs (1625–1666), who was employed by the British to protect their Caribbean colonies from Spanish, French and Dutch incursions. It is thought that Morgan participated in Admiral Myngs' successful sacking of Santiago de Cuba in 1662 and the daring raid on the Spanish fortification of Campeche (in modern-day southern Mexico) in 1663. Both of Myngs' raids on the Spanish reaped rich rewards and seem to have impressed the governor of Jamaica, Sir Thomas Modyford (1620–1679), as he issued Morgan with a letter of marque, which acted as a licence to conduct raids upon the ships of other countries and plunder the spoils – a proto-piracy licence, in effect.

As the relationship between England and Spain deteriorated, the possibility of a Spanish invasion of Jamaica became an ongoing concern. Although Modyford had been instructed by the Crown to curtail the activities of privateers, fear of Spanish reprisals led him to instruct Morgan 'to draw together the English privateers and take prisoners of the Spanish nation, whereby he might inform of the intention of that enemy to attack Jamaica, of which I have frequent and strong advice'. In short, Morgan's mission was to capture Spanish prisoners and torture them to try to obtain intelligence of any planned Spanish attack upon Jamaica.

Morgan's letter of marque only permitted him to engage Spanish ships at sea and did not cover attacks on Spanish-controlled ports and cities. As the terms and conditions of the letter of marque decreed that any plunder captured by Morgan should be split between the government and the people who leased their ships to the privateers, the profits from capturing Spanish ships and taking prisoners were likely to be quite negligible. Morgan, however, had other ideas, and having been newly promoted to the rank of admiral, in January 1668 he assembled a flotilla of twelve ships and an army of 700 men. Morgan's task force comprised a mix of buccaneers and ex-military men, at least a third of whom were enlisted from the French colony (and pirate stronghold) on the island of Tortuga. This mixture of English, French and Dutch soldiers of fortune made for an uneasy alliance. Morgan's plan was to attack mainland Spanish fortifications as the opportunities for plunder were greatly enhanced. As this was not included in his remit, and amounted to illegal piracy, any plunder taken did not have to be given over to the government and sponsors. Morgan relied upon the loophole that if he could convince Modyford that he had in fact acquired important intelligence (alongside considerable booty) then the governor would turn a blind eye to his acts of wanton piracy.

Initially Morgan planned to attack and ransack Havana, Cuba, but stealthy reconnaissance had revealed the port to be heavily fortified. Morgan turned his attention instead to Santa María del Puerto Príncipe (the modern-day Cuban city of Camagüey), a town 50 miles from the coast that Morgan correctly calculated would be poorly defended. Morgan and his men easily captured Puerto Príncipe but were disappointed to find very little in the way of treasure to plunder. According to Alexandre Exquemelin, who accompanied Morgan on the mission, 'It caused a general resentment and grief, to see such a small booty.'

With tensions running high between the English and French privateers (who felt they had been conned by their English counterparts), a fight broke out in which a French soldier was stabbed in the back. Morgan, mindful of a possible insurrection or mutiny, arrested the culprit and managed to placate the French contingent by promising the man would hang for his crime when they returned to Jamaica.

On arrival back at Port Royal, Jamaica, Morgan reported to Modyford that he had intelligence that a Spanish invasion force was gathering, with troops being sent from various Spanish colonies to rendezvous in Cuba. It is unclear if Morgan's information was accurate, or if this was just a ruse to cover up the fact that he had ignored his instruction only to attack Spanish ships in open water. It is also likely that Morgan, disappointed at the paltry gains from Puerto Príncipe, had his eyes on more lucrative targets and was using the fear of a Spanish invasion to persuade Modyford to sanction further missions.

In particular, Morgan's piratical gaze was taken with the city of Porto Bello in Panama – a key port on the Spanish trade route between the colonies and Europe. Although he had lost the support of the French privateers, who returned to Tortuga despite Morgan upholding his promise to hang the murderer of their countryman, Morgan was able to summon enough support to set sail for Panama in 1668.

Due to its importance as one of the principal Spanish trading posts, Porto Bello was heavily protected by three castles, two of which flanked the harbour, with a third fortification protecting the town. On 11 July 1668, Morgan dropped anchor in a cove some distance from Porto Bello and transferred his men into canoes, which they paddled several miles under cover of darkness to avoid detection. The element of surprise worked perfectly as Morgan and his men captured the town in a pincer movement by attacking from the flanks rather than head on, losing only an estimated twenty men in the mission and overpowering the Spanish who outnumbered the privateers five to one. The capture of Porto Bello is cited by scholars as evidence that Morgan was not only a ruthless opportunist but also a brilliant military strategist and commander.

Morgan and his men occupied Porto Bello for several weeks whilst they plundered whatever valuables they could find. Although it is likely that prisoners were tortured to extract information on hidden hoards of treasure, there is no evidence to support Exquemelin's account of wholesale rape and wanton cruelty towards the captured inhabitants. Morgan issued a ransom of 350,000 Spanish pesos for the city to Don Agustín, the Spanish governor of Panama, who responded by attempting to retake the city by force. Morgan and his men were able to repel the Spanish attack, but, keen to escape back to Jamaica with his considerable booty, a reduced ransom of 100,000 pesos was negotiated. Having secured the ransom and plundered the city, Morgan and his men returned to Port Royal with riches estimated to be worth between £70,000 and £100,000 (around £12 million in today's money). For their service each privateer received a sum of £120 from the booty, which amounted to several times their annual salary. Morgan awarded himself a considerably higher sum (thought to be in the region of £5,000), with Modyford receiving his obligatory 10 per cent share (£10,000) as per the conditions of Morgan's letter of marque. Morgan used part of his share of the treasure to buy two sugar plantations in Jamaica.

The Siege of Maracaibo

Emboldened by his successful raid on Porto Bello and eager for more riches, in October 1668 Morgan set sail with ten ships and 800 men for Île-à-Vache, a small island used as a rendezvous point by privateers. Morgan had hatched a plan to attack the Spanish settlement of Cartagena de Indias, on the northern coast of modern-day Colombia. Cartagena was Spain's richest city on mainland South America on account of being a main export point for silver; as a result it was heavily fortified and would take considerable firepower to successfully capture. Modyford loaned the *Oxford*, a Royal Navy frigate, to Morgan to use as his flagship, but a catastrophic explosion on board destroyed the warship before the raid could be undertaken. Although Morgan survived the blast, the loss of his flagship and over 200 men meant he no longer had the resources to attempt an ambitious attack on Cartagena.

On the advice of a French captain under his command, Morgan was persuaded to turn his attention to the Spanish settlements of Maracaibo and San Antonio de Gibraltar on the shores of Lake Maracaibo. The French privateer had participated in a raid on Maracaibo by the pirate François l'Olonnais (see The Real Pirates of the Caribbean: François l'Olonnais) in 1666 and knew how to navigate through the narrow entrances to the lagoon.

FIRST-HAND ACCOUNT OR FAKE NEWS?

The first account of Henry Morgan's exploits in the Caribbean was in the memoirs of his one-time comrade and surgeon, Alexandre Olivier Exquemelin. In his book *History of the Buccaneers of America* (1678), Exquemelin paints a less than flattering portrait of his former commander, accusing Morgan of extreme acts of pre-meditated cruelty and ruthlessness. In Exquemelin's version of the raid on Porto Bello, he describes how Morgan was able to capture the third fortification, which was set inland, by using captured prisoners as human shields. Morgan allegedly ordered the construction of extra-wide breaching ladders to scale the walls and 'commanded all the religious men and women whom he had taken prisoners to fix them against the walls of the castle ... these were forced, at the head of the companies to raise and apply them to the walls ... Thus many of the religious men and nuns were killed.'

When the book was published in English, Morgan took severe umbrage at Exquemelin's depiction of him, sued the author for libel and duly won (he was awarded £200 in damages), and as a result the section describing the use of monks and nuns as human shields was omitted from later editions of the book. However, other sections of Exquemelin's 'biography' remain intact, particularly accusations that Morgan and his men indulged in wholesale rape and torture of prisoners. There are no surviving Spanish accounts of Morgan's capture of Porto Bello to corroborate Exquemelin's claims (although some of Morgan's later missions pass reference to the use of torture).

Pirate scholars are divided on the veracity of Exquemelin's book, with one side arguing that it is a valuable and the only extant first-hand account of privateering and therefore can be taken as a genuine source, whilst others suggest the author held a long-standing grudge against his former commander (probably financial) and/or he 'sexed up' his account with lurid details to cause a sensation.

The use of torture in conflict is now outlawed by International Law and Morgan's actions, if true, would constitute war crimes in the modern day. However, in the seventeenth century torture was viewed by most European states as a legitimate military strategy.

PIRATE/BUCCANEER/PRIVATEER

As mentioned elsewhere, the lines distinguishing a 'pirate' from a 'buccaneer' and 'privateer' were frequently blurred during the so-called 'Golden Age' of piracy (circa mid-sixteenth to mid-seventeenth centuries). It is arguable that all privateers at this time engaged, willingly or otherwise, in acts of piracy. Or, to make the waters even muddier, privateers became buccaneers and vice versa. Put simply, you were a privateer if you were on the direct instruction of, and paid by, a sovereign state to undertake piratical activities. You were a buccaneer if you went it alone but often acted as a privateer when it suited you. Below, as succinctly as I can, are the different definitions as far as I understand them, but I'm probably wrong:

Pirate: A person who unlawfully relieves people(s) of their property and possessions by means of a sailing vessel. Piracy is as old as the hills and has carried the death penalty in many countries dating back to Ancient Egypt.

Buccaneer: The name buccaneer dates from early French settlers on the island of Hispaniola in the seventeenth century. As Spanish interest in Hispaniola had been neglected in favour of their frenzied search for gold, parts of the island became home, or a relatively safe haven, for all number of wanderers from deserting soldiers to escaped slaves and deported criminals. These vagabond hordes had to hunt for food, but thankfully wild cattle and boars were plentiful, and they would smoke the meat on wooden frames called *boucans*. Perhaps slightly unkindly, they were given the nickname *boucaniers* (in French) or buccaneers in English. Eventually the Spanish began to realise that a large part of one of their colonies, which although not financially profitable in their eyes, was of strategic value in the New World bunfight, drove the *boucaniers* to Tortuga. Henry Morgan and others, knowing of the *boucaniers'* fighting skills and nautical prowess, would then enlist them as part of an army of, you guessed it, privateers. This is not to say that buccaneers weren't prone to going rogue, but in the main they were pirates for hire.

Privateer: A sailor/soldier granted an official government licence (known as letter of marque in English) to attack an enemy of his country in times of war or diplomatic unrest who in return could keep the plunder on condition of paying the government a certain percentage. This was by no means a British construct, and both the French and the Dutch governments and organisations made extensive use of privateers. The Dutch West India Company had an entire army of privateers on their payroll and the French embraced the concept to the extent that the ports of

St-Malo and Dieppe were privateering labour exchanges. Rock up to the port and get in a couple of fights and someone would give you a job.

The exploits of France's most famous pirate/privateer, Jean Bart, became so much a part of Dieppe folklore that a statue was erected in his honour. The statue survived the blanket bombing of the port during the Second World War and still stands to this day. In the sixteenth and seventeenth centuries, privateers if captured in skirmishes were punished as pirates by their enemies. The Spanish, with some justification, saw no distinction between legitimate soldier and pirate, and Christopher Columbus was detained on charges of piracy by his own countrymen on more than one occasion. However, during the eighteenth century, privateers came to be viewed as lawful combatants who could be kept prisoner and used as collateral bargaining chips rather than just strung up from the nearest tree. Nevertheless, as with buccaneers, the line between legal contract soldier and flagrant pirate was a thin one, with the use of privateers (supposedly) being outlawed across most of Europe in the mid-nineteenth century.

Maracaibo was protected by the star fort of San Carlos de la Barra Fortress, 20 miles (32km) outside the city, on the approach across the lake. Although strategically in an excellent position to defend the town, the Spanish had left only a handful of soldiers to man the battlements and twelve large cannon.

Under covering cannon fire from their battleships, Morgan and his men landed on the beach and stormed the fortification only to find it had been deserted. The fleeing Spanish soldiers had left behind a crude booby trap of gunpowder kegs, intended to destroy the fortress when it was breached, but Morgan and his men diffused the device before spiking the cannon to avoid them being used against their ships on the return journey.

On arrival in Maracaibo, Morgan found the city had been deserted as the inhabitants had been forewarned of the impending attack and had fled into the surrounding jungle. Morgan's men searched the area and rounded up deserters who they tortured to find where money or valuables had been stashed. Morgan spent three weeks ransacking and pillaging whatever he could find in Maracaibo before sailing on across the lake to San Antonio de Gibraltar.

On arrival at Gibraltar, Morgan was met with more resistance from the town's occupants than he had encountered at Maracaibo. The residents refused to surrender, and the fortification had enough firepower to keep Morgan's ships at bay. Morgan deployed the same stealth tactics that had served him handsomely in the mission to Porto Bello the previous year and dispatched a landing party by canoes to capture the town. Morgan and his men spent five weeks ransacking Gibraltar and there was again evidence that torture was used to force residents to reveal hidden money and treasure.

When Morgan returned to Maracaibo they received news that a large Spanish defence fleet had arrived and was waiting for them in the narrow channel at the mouth of Lake Maracaibo. The Spanish had also reclaimed and rearmed the guns at the San Carlos de la Barra Fortress. In short, Morgan and his men were cornered with their escape route back to Jamaica blocked. The Armada de Barlovento was a formidable naval fleet under the command of Admiral Don Alonso del Campo y Espinosa, who had been personally dispatched by the King of Spain to track Morgan down and bring him to justice for his attacks on Cuba and Panama the previous year. Don Alonso had at his disposal the pride of the Spanish fleet, *Magdalen* – a veritable dreadnought of a warship armed with forty-six huge cannon and backed up by several other large battleships. The Spanish had enough firepower to easily blow Morgan and his men out of the water.

Don Alonso was a man of military principle, however, and although he had the upper hand and would surely overpower Morgan's fleet in open-water conflict, he recognised that his fleet would inevitably incur losses into the bargain. Morgan sent a delegation to negotiate with Don Alonso and offered to free all the prisoners he had in captivity and refrain from burning Maracaibo to the ground in return for safe passage across the lake.

Don Alonso rejected Morgan's somewhat risible attempt at a deal and returned with a counter offer that Morgan and his men relinquish all of the plunder and release the prisoners in return for freedom to escape to Jamaica. According to

Exquemelin, Morgan gathered all his men at a meeting in the marketplace at Maracaibo and put the Spanish offer to a vote. Morgan's men, perhaps fearing the Spanish would double-cross them, voted overwhelmingly to fight their way out or perish in the process rather than relinquish their spoils.

Morgan and his captains formed a war council and drew up a devious plan of escape that centred on a clever deception. Morgan calculated that the key to their chances of escape was to find a way to take out *Magdalen* – the centrepiece of the Spaniards' firepower.

Twelve of Morgan's men prepared a small Spanish frigate they had commandeered in Gibraltar and dressed the deck up with disguised logs of wood and dummies to make the ship look fully crewed. They also cut additional holes in the hull to resemble extra cannon. Morgan's plan was to use his counterfeit warship as a fireship and float her into *Magdalen*. To this end, barrels of powder were placed in the ship and grappling irons laced into the ships rigging, to catch the ropes and sails of *Magdalen* and ensure the vessels would become entangled.

On 1 May, Morgan and his fleet attacked the Spanish Armada and his fireship plan was a spectacular success. Not only was *Magdalen* set on fire, she was abandoned and sank in Maracaibo bay. Morgan and his men also captured the imposing thirty-six-cannon warship *Soledad* and sank a further two Spanish ships. Don Alonso and his wounded men retreated to the San Carlos de la Barra Fortress, calculating that Morgan's ships would still have to sail past the fortress to escape and that the cannon on the battlements were easily sufficient to destroy the privateer's fleet. Although Morgan had won a memorable battle, he and his men were still, to all intents and purposes, trapped and so he attempted to negotiate again with Don Alonso who, having seen the pride of his fleet go up in flames, was in no mood whatsoever to strike a deal. Morgan turned instead to the citizens of Maracaibo and negotiated a ransom for the city of 20,000 pesos and 500 head of cattle in return for not burning the city and releasing prisoners.

Morgan sent reconnaissance to San Carlos de la Barra Fortress who reported back that Don Alonso had reset the cannon on the battlements to point landward, suggesting that the Spanish were expecting Morgan and his men to attack by land. Morgan then sent a fake landing force towards the fortress to dupe the Spanish into preparing for a land battle and waited for the cover of darkness and the tide to change. When darkness fell, Morgan and his fleet raised anchor but did not unfurl their sails and quietly sneaked past the fortress and drifted out into the lake before the Spanish could recalibrate the guns.

Morgan and his men's daring escape from Maracaibo was further evidence of his military acumen and cunning, and the privateers were handsomely rewarded with a considerable bounty, having looted the ill-fated *Magdalen* before they left. However, they returned to Jamaica to find that the British government was in the process of negotiating with the Spanish Crown and Modyford had been instructed by Charles II to rebuke Morgan for overstepping his remit and to revoke his letter of marque (privateer's/pirate's licence). The privateers were allowed to keep the majority of their plunder, with Morgan investing his share in further sugar plantations on Jamaica.

The Attack on Panama

Attempts at establishing a peace accord between England and Spain faltered, possibly on account of Morgan's and other privateers' activities in the Caribbean. In 1669 Mariana, the Queen Regent of Spain, ordered attacks on English shipping in the Caribbean. The Spanish, who had been slow on the uptake of employing privateers to protect their interests, began a series of tit-for-tat attacks on English trade ships in 1670.

In retaliation, Modyford re-issued letters of marque to Morgan with the instruction 'to do and perform all manner of exploits, which may tend to the preservation and quiet of this island'. Morgan needed no further encouragement and set about assembling the largest army of privateers ever noted in the Caribbean at that time. A fleet of over thirty English and French ships carrying several thousand men set sail for the Spanish-controlled mainland. Morgan's fleet stopped first at Old Providence and Santa Catalina, two Spanish outposts that are part of modern-day Colombia. After restocking with equipment and supplies, the fleet sailed to Chagres, a key trade outpost from which goods were transported from Spanish South America back to Europe. Morgan captured the town and occupied Fort San Lorenzo, a strategically placed fortification at the mouth of the Chagres river, which was the access channel to Old Panama City. Morgan stationed a garrison at the fort to protect his line of retreat, mindful not to get trapped again. Taking the remainder of his men, Morgan continued on foot and by canoe through the dense rainforests and swamps of the isthmus, fighting off Spanish ambushes along the way.

Morgan's army of privateers arrived at Old Panama City on 27 January 1671 to find that the Spanish governor had been forewarned of an impending attack and had assembled a considerable defence force of 1,500 men. Morgan, although outnumbered, again displayed his military prowess by skilfully outmanoeuvring the Spanish infantry and luring them into a trap. In a bizarre attempt to disorientate Morgan's men, the governor of Panama released two herds of oxen and bulls on to the battlefield. However, the animals got spooked by the sound of the gunfire and stampeded over the Spanish lines of defence, enabling Morgan's troops to break through. Although the battle was a crushing defeat for the Spanish, who lost in the region of 500 men in comparison to only fifteen privateers killed, the governor ordered the city to be burned to the ground to avoid being plundered.

The fires raged for several days, largely destroying the city in the process, although much of the wealth had been removed before Morgan and his men arrived. Nonetheless, Morgan spent three weeks gathering together whatever plunder he could find, although, due to the scale of the mission, the share apportioned to his men was modest and, according to Exquemelin, caused discontent among the troops.

When Morgan returned to Jamaica he discovered that Charles II had signed the Treaty of Madrid: an agreement with Spain to allow English ships freedom of movement in the Caribbean in return for the suppression of piracy/privateering. Both Modyford and Morgan had been unaware of the king's sudden volte-face (the treaty had been signed prior to the raid on Panama) and their actions had enraged the Spanish and embarrassed the English Crown. In order to avoid any escalating conflict, Modyford was removed as governor and he and Morgan were ordered back to England to account for their actions.

It is unclear if the recalling of Modyford and Morgan was a token gesture to appease the Spanish, or part of the conditions of the treaty. Either way, Morgan's exploits had seen his reputation rise to that of a folk hero in the eyes of the public, which probably saved him from any notable punishment.

From Pirate to Politician: Morgan's Last Years

After two years back in England, the policy of appeasement with Spain had attracted some criticism, and concerns were voiced over the suitability of Jamaica's defences should the Spanish renege on the treaty. Modyford's replacement as governor of Jamaica, Sir Thomas Lynch (?–1684), had caused unrest on the island by revoking all letters of marque, and in 1674 Charles II appointed Lord Carberry (1639–1713) as his replacement, with Morgan to act as deputy. King Charles also appointed Morgan a Knight Bachelor – a low-ranking knight of the realm.

Morgan's remit, ironically, was to curtail piracy and reinforce Jamaica's defences. On arrival back in Port Royal, Morgan was voted on to the Assembly of Jamaica (the island's governing body) and awarded an annual salary of £600 – a move opposed by the new governor, Carberry, with whom Morgan had a frosty relationship.

Although letters of marque had been revoked, Jamaica remained at the pivot of privateering in the Caribbean, which placed Morgan in a compromising position. Morgan had close relationships with many privateers, both personally and professionally (he had financial investments in several privateer ships), and this was a cause of concern to Carberry. Although Morgan had no authority to issue letters of marque, he used his contacts with the French, notably the governor of Tortuga, to find a loophole whereby privateers could continue to go about their business, albeit in an unofficial capacity. Carberry wrote in a letter to the Secretary of State that he had become 'every day more convinced of ... [Morgan's] imprudence and unfitness to have anything to do with civil government' and reported that Morgan spent much time with undesirables 'drinking and gaming at the Taverns'.

In July 1676, Carberry attempted unsuccessfully to oust Morgan from his position as deputy governor by calling a meeting of the Assembly of Jamaica and accusing Morgan of collaborating with French privateers to attack Spanish interests in the Caribbean. However, Morgan had powerful allies on the Assembly who voted instead to have Carberry removed and sent back to England. Morgan subsequently served as governor for several months until a new appointment arrived from London.

Carberry and former governor Thomas Lynch continued to conspire against Morgan with Lynch eventually paying Charles II £50,000 to have Morgan removed from office and relieved of his duties. Morgan had been a heavy drinker for many years and the effects were taking a serious toll on his health.

Morgan never regained his positions of power and influence in Jamaica and continued to drink heavily, causing further decline in his health. In 1687, Christopher Monck, Second Duke of Albemarle (1653–1688), was appointed governor of Jamaica. Albemarle was sympathetic towards Morgan and successfully petitioned James II to reinstate him to the Assembly. Morgan, however, was too ill to take up an active role and Albemarle instructed his private physician, Sir Hans Sloane, to examine him and diagnose the cause of his illness. Sloane described Morgan in his journal as:

> ... lean, sallow-coloured, his eyes a little yellowish and belly jutting out or prominent ... He complained to me of want of appetite for victuals, he had a kicking ... to vomit every morning and generally a small looseness attending him, and withal is much given to drinking and sitting up late, which I supposed had been the cause of his present indisposition.

Sir Henry 'Captain' Morgan died from complications related to his alcoholism on 25 August 1688 aged 53. Albemarle ordered a state funeral and issued an amnesty so fellow pirates and privateers could pay their last respects. Morgan left behind a considerable estate, including three sugar plantations with refineries and distilleries and several hundred slaves alongside a considerable personal fortune. Several places on Jamaica are named after Morgan, who was a key figure in early Jamaican history. However, it is perhaps the brand of rum bearing his name that remains his most enduring legacy, which is ironic given it was his thirst for alcohol that caused his death.

Mount Gay 1703 Black Barrel

Mount Gay is reputed to be the oldest surviving rum distillery in the world, with deeds dating to 1703, and lists in its inventory 'one mill house, seven coppers, one curing house and one still house'. Originally a sugar refinery named Mount Gilboa, the estate was created by William Sandiford (dates unknown) by amalgamating several existing sugar plantations in the St Lucy region of Barbados. In 1747 the sugar mill and presumably the accompanying distillery were sold by the Sandiford family to John Sober who subsequently employed Sir John Gay Alleyne (1724–1801), the owner of the nearby St Nicholas Abbey plantation, to run the estate for the Sober family. Alleyne was a prominent figure on Barbados and a skilful businessman. In 1757, Alleyne was elected for the Parish of St Andrew to the Parliament of Barbados, a seat he held for the next forty years, including a lengthy term as Speaker of the House of Assembly of Barbados between 1767 and 1779.

Alleyne, a descendent of the early settlers on Barbados, had a progressive outlook towards the island's politics. He publicly voiced opinions unpopular with the plantation class at the time, declaring in the House of Assembly that he disapproved of the system of slavery: 'an unhappy sight which leaves an immense debt upon us to clear the obligation of human nature.' Alleyne also established the Seminary – a school for the impoverished that admitted both white and black children. Sir John Alleyne was also successful in business and it is believed he was the mover and shaker behind expanding the plantation's distillery business as a means of maximising the estate's output. On his death in 1801, the Sober family renamed the company Mount Gay in his honour.

Mount Gay's rums exemplify the Bajan style of rum. Whereas Jamaica is synonymous with heavier pot-still blends, the Barbados approach blends both pot-still and column-still marques. Mount Gay's signature blend The Eclipse was first launched in 1910 and remains one of the best budget-priced rums on the market. The Eclipse was named after the total solar eclipse that occurred in 1910 and in honour of the passing of Halley's Comet the same year.

Although more difficult to find on the shelves of supermarkets, Mount Gay Black Barrel is a beautiful oaky rum, blended from both pot and column stills but containing a higher ratio of pot-stilled spirit. It is a beautifully coloured rum, courtesy of an extra maturation period after blending in heavily toasted bourbon casks. Mount Gay Black Barrel has soothing hints of honey and caramel with a smoky tobacco finish.

The Mount Gay estate still owns its own sugar plantations from which they can yield up to 6,000 tons of molasses per year for their rums. One other unique selling point of all Mount Gay rums is that they source the water for their rum washes from their own underground wells on the estate where it is filtered through coral and limestone.

The Real Pirates of the Caribbean: François l'Olonnais

François l'Olonnais (circa 1630–1669) was a French privateer who earned the reputation of being the most sadistic and bloodthirsty of all seventeenth-century pirates, operating for around ten years until he himself came to a sticky end. Nicknamed the 'Flail of Spain' for his particularly ferocious hatred of the Spanish, l'Olonnais was an astute and fearless marauder who showed no mercy to his captives.

Jean-David Nau was born around 1630 in Les Sables-d'Olonne, a coastal town in western France, to a penniless family who sold him, at the age of 15, to work as an indentured servant on a sugar plantation in Martinique. From there he was transferred to the Spanish-run island of Hispaniola (Haiti and the Dominican Republic) where he toiled for ten years under brutal conditions before he was finally released (or, according to some sources, possibly escaped earlier). The harsh treatment he received from his masters obviously had a deep effect on Jean-David, leading to his lifelong loathing of the Spanish to the extent that he took every opportunity to inflict pain and suffering upon them.

After leaving the plantation, rather than returning to France, he stayed on in the Caribbean and joined the mainly French and English buccaneers stationed in the French colony of St-Domingue, who often targeted the Spanish colonists. He began to develop a reputation for ruthlessness and saw this as an opportunity to exact revenge on the Spanish whenever he could, and so he joined the crew of a ship full of fellow buccaneers in search of riches and revenge. He quickly became well known for his vindictive and violent acts, thinking nothing of slicing flesh from those he disliked or removing the tongue of anyone who dared to offend him.

By this time, having changed his name to François l'Olonnais, his natural aptitude as a buccaneer had been recognised by Monsieur de la Place, the French governor of Tortuga (an island off the north-west coast of Hispaniola), who placed him in command of a small ship. It is said that he brought a priest on board ship to bless his new crew and that, when one of the men started heckling during the prayer, l'Olonnais wasted no time in shooting the offender and throwing him into the sea.

l'Olonnais now had an official letter from the French government authorising him to attack and plunder any Spanish ship he encountered, and he took his work very seriously, taking every opportunity to obliterate the Spanish whilst enjoying a profitable career. His terrifying reputation grew, as he mercilessly slew all those on board the ships he captured, often pointlessly torturing them in the process. However, around 1663, his ship was wrecked near the Campeche in Mexico, and although he and his men survived this, they were unlucky to encounter a party of Spanish soldiers. Most of the crew were wiped out but somehow l'Olonnais managed to avoid death and evade capture by smothering himself with the blood of his fallen crew and hiding amongst their bodies. Once the Spanish had departed, he disguised himself as a Spaniard and made his way to Campeche where he persuaded some French slaves to assist him before making his way back to Tortuga, and henceforth continued to terrorise the Spanish. Shortly after this incident, he and his new crew held a town hostage demanding a ransom from its

Spanish rulers. A ship was detailed by the governor of Havana with specific instructions to annihilate l'Olonnais and his party, but instead l'Olonnais captured and beheaded every one of the Spaniards bar one, whom he only spared so that he could deliver a message to Havana: 'I shall never henceforward give quarter to any Spaniard whatsoever.'

Not only was l'Olonnais barbaric, he was also clever and is known for being one of the first buccaneers to conduct land raids. In 1666 he joined forces with Michel le Basque (?–1668), a fellow buccaneer, and sailed from Tortuga with a crew of 440 pirates to sack the city of Maracaibo. En route they came across and captured a Spanish ship carrying a cargo of cocoa beans, gemstones and more than 260,000 Spanish dollars before formulating a plan to capture the allegedly impregnable city.

Lake Maracaibo sat at the entrance to the city, which was defended by the San Carlos de la Barra Fortress and its twelve guns, making an attack by sea almost impossible. Therefore, l'Olonnais decided to advance on it overland and seize the city at a point where it was undefended. The marauders took Maracaibo in a few hours, but as they ransacked the city they realised that most of the residents had escaped and had either taken their gold with them or hidden it. So l'Olonnais tracked them down and mercilessly tortured them until they revealed its whereabouts. Having accomplished their task, they destroyed most of the city's defensive walls, ensuring their speedy retreat.

l'Olonnais adopted a hands-on approach to torture and liked to be personally involved in developing barbarous techniques with which to inflict the maximum amount of pain and terror on his victims, which included slicing lumps of flesh from his prey, burning them alive, and even tying knotted rope around their heads so tightly that their eyes were forced out.

After sacking Maracaibo, l'Olonnais moved on to San Antonio de Gibraltar and, despite being outnumbered, his men wiped out 500 Spanish soldiers and held Gibraltar to ransom. The ransom was duly paid (20,000 pieces of eight and 500 cattle), but, obviously a man not to be trusted, despite the payment he went on to ransack the entire city, stealing 260,000 pieces of eight, gems, silverware, silks and a number of slaves.

On his final expedition, in 1668, l'Olonnais recruited 700 men and six ships with the aim of reaching the coast of Nicaragua. However, after being blown off course, they arrived at the Gulf of Honduras where they proceeded to raid the Spanish settlements around the area, but the exercise turned out to be relatively unprofitable. The party then moved on to the town of San Pedro, situated close to a Spanish gold mine, but they came under attack several times and lost a considerable number of men. These skirmishes continued until l'Olonnais managed to capture some unfortunate Spanish soldiers whom he interrogated as to whether there were unguarded routes to the gold mine. The prisoners refused to cooperate, whereupon l'Olonnais committed his most infamous act of depravity: slicing open the chest of one Spaniard, he pulled out his heart and proceeded to chew on it. Unsurprisingly, the remaining hostages immediately became compliant and gave him the information he had requested. However, San Pedro did not prove to be as lucrative as he had thought and, disillusioned by his recent lack of success, many of his party began to desert him.

With his remaining crew, l'Olonnais set off again in an attempt to reach Nicaragua, but the ship ran aground on the cost of Darien (Panama) and, being unable to relaunch the ship, they were forced to set off on foot to find food. The party were captured by the indigenous Kuna tribe, who killed l'Olonnais, tearing him limb from limb and, according to some sources, cannibalising him. In *History of the Buccaneers of America* (1684) Alexandre Exquemelin writes that the Kuma '... tore him in pieces alive, throwing his body limb by limb into the fire and his ashes into the air; to the intent no trace nor memory might remain of such an infamous, inhuman creature'.

PART 3

THE REVOLUTIONARY SPIRIT

RUM IN NORTH AMERICA, RUM
RUNNING DURING PROHIBITION AND
THE AUSTRALIAN RUM REBELLION

Rum in North America: The Fuel of a Revolution?

The United States of America, in terms of spirits, is renowned as the home of whiskey bourbon. Indeed, in 1964 the American Congress passed a law protecting 'America's native spirit', prohibiting any product not distilled in the US from calling itself bourbon. However, in historical terms at least, it is rum that is arguably the true spirit of America.

Following rum's, albeit fairly slow, development in the Caribbean, it spread rapidly to British colonies in North America. There are various theories, both social and economic, as to the reasons why the American colonists embraced rum on a scale that rivalled the 'gin craze' in England in the first half of the eighteenth century.

The first recorded distillery in the US was built on Staten Island in 1650, with further distilleries springing up in Massachusetts and New England soon after. The early colonists had experienced little success with establishing goods or commodities that could be effectively traded and, like the Spanish, suffered at the hands of fluctuations in the tobacco market in Europe. The burgeoning demand for sugar in Europe had resulted in a huge surplus of molasses across the Caribbean. Some was distilled into rum for consumption by the locals and found its way on to privateers' ships, but there was only limited exportation of rum to Europe at this time. Plantation owners had a problem with what to do with the excess molasses left over from industrial sugar production – there is only so much of the sticky goo that can be fed to animals and slaves.

It is thought that it was an enterprising Dutch trader who first exported barrels of molasses to the fledgling colonies of America. One can imagine the conversation on the quay as large quantities of the stuff were unloaded: 'What the hell are we supposed to do with that?'

'Its okay,' says the Dutchman, producing a copper still, 'I'll show you.'

However it came about, the fledgling colonies in North America had found a product that they could produce and trade on the infamous Trade Triangle.

The earliest attempts to profit from the northern colonies had been less than successful. The first settlers were not particularly skilled and barely able to survive, let alone produce profitable exports for their sponsors in Europe. The raw materials on hand, such as wood and stone, were widely available in England, and attempts at manufactured goods, such as glass and textiles, were not encouraging. One area the early American settlers did excel in was metalwork. Every settlement had several skilled blacksmiths and these artisans were soon able to turn their hand to making copper stills for distilleries. New England and Massachusetts were also abundant in oak and maple trees for making barrels, and so they had the raw materials for producing and storing rum.

The Big Sugar Act Squeeze

Within a few decades of the establishment of the first Staten Island distillery, rum was being produced all across the North

American colonies. The steady increases in the migrant population inevitably led to a level of demand for rum that was outstripping supply from local producers. The need for more rum meant the need for greater shipments of molasses from the Caribbean.

Britain maintained patronising attitudes towards its colonial cousins in North America, regarding them with an indifference bordering upon contempt. The colonies were, notionally at least, prohibited from trading with anyone other than British Caribbean colonies, leaving the British plantations with a monopoly on selling the much sought-after molasses. The British set a price of around 10 pence (approximately £5 in today's money) for a barrel of molasses from the Caribbean plantations, which initially the rum producers of New England and Massachusetts seemed happy enough to pay. However, as the colonists started to get their act together with other products and commodities, particularly grain, livestock and cotton, the protectionism that banned the sale of goods to Britain (intended to protect domestic business) began to bite the colonists.

The rum producers of North America, eager to find a better deal for molasses, turned their attention on the sly to other parts of the Caribbean. Although rum was distilled in French colonies such as Haiti, Martinique and Guadeloupe, the French preference was for *rhum agricole*, a spirit distilled from cane juice. This left the French plantations with a huge excess of molasses, which was finding its way back to ports on mainland France in huge quantities. If it was British protectionism stifling North America's trading options, French protectionism became its saviour.

THE TRADE TRIANGLE :
THE MIDDLE PASSAGE

The discovery of 'the middle passage' – a route across the Atlantic from the coast of West Africa – by Portuguese navigators in the fifteenth century gave rise to the first Trade Triangle between Europe, Africa and the New World of the Americas. The Portuguese had maintained a virtual monopoly on slave trading since the mid-fifteenth century, but by the seventeenth century, and the establishment of the Caribbean and American colonies, other European powers got in on the act.

The first leg of the triangle was known as the 'outward passage'. European ships were loaded with manufactured goods such as textiles, ironware, gunpowder and weapons, which set sail for Africa from Europe for 'slave ports' such as Ouidah and Lagos. On arrival, the European goods were traded for slaves who had been kidnapped from central Africa by tribal chieftains from Nigeria, Angola and the Ivory Coast.

The 'middle passage' was the harrowing second leg of the triangle in which slaves were chained and packed on to ships for the four-to-six-week voyage across the Atlantic to the colonies. Conditions on board were hellish, with slaves packed into tiny spaces only a few feet wide. Unsurprisingly, the captive, terrified Africans, many of whom would never have seen the sea before, let alone travelled on a ship, were prone to contract diseases such as measles, yellow fever and typhoid. Aware that on average at least a third of their 'cargo' was unlikely to survive the journey, the traders attempted to compensate for any loses by overcrowding their ships, which if anything made the possibility of disease on an epidemic scale all the more likely. In his memoir *The Interesting Narrative*, first published in 1789, Nigerian-born slave and writer Olaudah Equiano (circa 1745–1797) describes the conditions on the slave ship that transported him, aged 11, from Lagos to Barbados in the mid 1750s: '... the closeness of the place, and the heat of the climate, added to the numbers in the ship was suffocating ... The shrieks of the women and the groans of the dying, rendered the whole a scene of horror almost inconceivable.'

On arrival in the Americas, the surviving slaves – sick, malnourished and traumatised – were sold at auction and put to work on the plantations. The revenue from the human cargo was then reinvested in commodities such as sugar, coffee, spices, cotton and rum, which were then transported via 'the inward passage' back to Europe. This triangular trade system of goods in exchange for exploited human labour is often cited as the beginning of a system of global capitalism.

The French government, under pressure from the powerful wine and brandy lobbies, passed a law prohibiting the import of *rhum agricole* and molasses to mainland France. However, rather shrewdly they virtually abandoned re-export tariffs for exports of molasses to other countries. This enabled the North Americans to import molasses from the French Caribbean islands for almost half the price the British plantation owners were charging. It also paved the way for the North American colonies to trade other commodities with the French islands, including cotton, timber and particularly fish from the waters around New England and Newfoundland, for which there was great demand in the French colonial Caribbean. By 1730, North America was importing 90 per cent of its molasses from the French, whose government passed a law, by way of compensating the plantation owners, that molasses could only be exchanged for fish.

Unsurprisingly, the British plantation owners, having lost out on a useful burgeoning market for molasses, complained to the British government. As a result of their lobbying, the British government passed the Molasses Act of 1733, which imposed import taxes on molasses purchased from French or Dutch colonies. The effect of the tax was to bring the price of molasses on a par with what the British colonies had originally been charging America, thereby eliminating any favourable conditions from buying from elsewhere.

This interference in America's flourishing rum industry was not taken lying down by the distillers of North America. They found ingenious ways to avoid paying the tax, including forging import bills by passing molasses off as other products and basically smuggling it, by a variety of devious means, into American ports undetected. This refusal to pay the molasses tax allowed the American rum industry to flourish and provided the colonists with a commodity that they too could trade on the Second Trade Triangle that sprang up between Africa, the Caribbean and North America. Moreover, it showed the colonists had started to stand on their own feet and refused to be bullied by the British government. A small seedling of dissent had been sown that would eventually explode at the Boston Tea Party and ignite the American Revolutionary War.

In truth, the British government had been somewhat slack when enforcing the Molasses Act and for several decades the revenue raised had a negligible impact on the nation's coffers. However, Britain's involvement in the Seven Years War (1756–1763) had been a costly enterprise and plunged the country into debt (the debt had grown from £75,000,000 before the war to £122,600,000 in January 1763, and almost £130,000,000 by the beginning of 1764).

The thirty-year-old Molasses Act was due to expire in 1763 and the British government anticipated an increase in demand for rum, particularly as Britain had now taken control of Canada. The British Prime Minister, John Stuart, the Earl of Bute, had proposed maintaining a military force in North America to protect British interests and needed to find a means to fund it. Bute's successor, George Grenville, proposed and passed through parliament an updated version of the Molasses Act in 1764, ostensibly to raise funds to pay for the British defence force in North America.

The Sugar Act, although actually reducing the taxation on molasses by 50 per cent, was subjected to far greater implementation than its predecessor. The British government was determined to clamp down on smuggling and took various measures to ensure effective collection of revenue, including sending a fleet of thirty Royal Navy ships to police the seaways. Other taxes were placed upon certain goods and commodities, most notably lumber that could only be exported to Britain, effectively outlawing any trade with the French Caribbean islands. Ships' captains were required to maintain detailed manifests of their cargo and the papers were subjected to verification before anything could be unloaded from the ships. Customs officials were empowered to have all violations tried in Vice Admiralty courts rather than by jury trials in local colonial courts, where the juries generally looked favourably on smuggling as a profession and part and parcel of free-market commerce and not a capital offence punishable by hanging.

The Sugar Act was met with considerable consternation by the colonists and sparked widespread protests. During the Seven Years War the mainstay of the colonial economy had been supplying food and supplies to the British Army and hence the end of the war had resulted in an economic downturn. Prior to the act the American rum industry was thriving, producing some 6 million gallons per annum, 80 per cent of which was manufactured with imported molasses from the French and Dutch West Indies.

The New England ports and distilleries particularly suffered economic losses from the implementation of the Sugar Act as the stricter legal enforcement made smuggling molasses more perilous. The rum producers and traders argued that the profit margins on rum were too slight to justify taxation on molasses and this would force a marked increase in prices that could not be sustained. The British West Indies, on the other hand, now had undivided access to colonial exports. With supply of molasses well exceeding demand, the islands prospered with their reduced expenses while New England ports saw revenue from their rum exports decrease. As colonial discontent and protests increased, the anti-Sugar Act movement was galvanised by future 'Founding Father' Samuel Adams and lawyer and activist James Otis. In May 1764 Samuel Adams drafted a report on the Sugar Act for the Massachusetts assembly in which he denounced the act as an infringement of the rights of the colonists as British subjects:

> For if our Trade may be taxed why not our Lands? Why not the Produce of our Lands & everything we possess or make use of? This we apprehend annihilates our Charter Right to govern & tax ourselves – It strikes our British privileges, which as we have never forfeited them, we hold in common with our fellow subjects who are natives of Britain: If taxes are laid upon us in any shape without our having a legal representation where they are laid, are we not reduced from the character of free subjects to the miserable state of tributary slaves?

Adams' report is notable because it contains reference to what would become the rallying cry of the colonial Patriots: 'taxation without representation is tyranny'. Adams had moved the argument away from an analysis of the economic effects of the Sugar Act and focused instead on constitutional issues. Under the British Bill of Rights 1689, the government

GEORGE WASHINGTON'S RUM OBSESSION

Rum continued to be produced and consumed in large quantities in America up to and after the American Revolutionary War (1775–1783). The first President of the United States George Washington (1732–1799) was a keen rum connoisseur. In 1751, Washington accompanied his elder brother Lawrence on a trip to Barbados – the only time he travelled outside America. Lawrence was riddled with tuberculosis and it was thought the change of climate might aid his recovery. Whilst on Barbados, Washington contracted smallpox, which left a lasting blemish on his skin, but he put his recovery from the disease down to drinking Bajan rum.

When Washington first entered politics in 1757 he stood against two other candidates in Frederick County, Virginia. It was common practice in Virginia elections to 'buy' votes by serving alcohol at hustings – a practice that Washington disapproved of. Suffice to say he gained only 7 per cent of the vote and suffered the only electoral defeat of his long and distinguished political career. However, undeterred, Washington stood for election again the following year and plied voters with 28 gallons of rum, 50 gallons of rum punch, 46 gallons of beer and 34 gallons of wine. The ploy worked as Washington was comfortably elected by his somewhat merry supporters.

Rum also played an important role whilst Washington acted as Commander-in-Chief during the Revolutionary War. Rum rations were distributed to his soldiers to boost morale and he also ordered large quantities to be stockpiled for medicinal use as an anaesthetic by battlefield surgeons. There are several mentions of rum in Washington's letter and journals during the war where he frets that rum supplies are running low and this could have a severe impact on the Patriots' chances of victory.

It is fitting then that at his inauguration on 30 April 1789 in New York, Washington ordered a large shipment of high-grade rum to be imported from Barbados to be drunk in celebration of the historic moment.

cannot tax its subjects without their consent – that is to say, the consent of the people provided by virtue of an elected assembly. As the colonists provided no Members of Parliament and therefore had no elected representatives to protect or advance their interests, they were not giving their 'consent' to be taxed: the taxes were constitutionally invalid.

The response of the British government to the growing unrest in the colonies was mixed. On one hand there was a lobby who felt that the colonies were not a Crown dependency and that the need to raise revenue and show them who was in charge was paramount as to back down would set a precedent. On the other hand, there was a lobby who were concerned that damage to trade relations between Britain and America could prove financially damaging in the future (over fifty New York traders had signed a boycott on importing British luxury goods in support of repealing the Sugar Act). Two years after its implementation, the Sugar Act was repealed and replaced by the Revenue Act, which reduced the taxation on molasses to 1 pence per barrel and lifted the embargo on importing molasses from the French Caribbean. However, the government introduced the Stamp Act at the same time – a proto-taxation on paper that enraged the colonists even more than the Sugar Act had done, causing widespread organised protests.

Rum suffered a decline in America as spectacularly as its emergence after the American Civil War. The abolition of slavery undoubtedly had a huge effect but also the development of the American bourbon industry. As American agriculture expanded, the taste for grain-based spirits increased – there was little point importing molasses to distil to make spirits when there were the raw materials on their doorstep. The imposition of Prohibition saw rum briefly rise again in the 1920s, albeit under largely illicit circumstances, but it is only since the turn of the twenty-first century that a taste for rum has re-emerged in America. Sales are increasing at a rapid rate and small-batch distillers and marques are springing up (see Rums of Distinction: Bad Bitch Spanish Marie).

Ironically, the rise and regulation of American bourbon had a knock-on effect on rum production in the Caribbean, in a reversal of fortunes. Whereas originally Caribbean sugar plantations off-loaded their excess resources of molasses to the New England rum distilleries, the dictate that bourbon barrels can only be filled once during ageing means there is a ready supply of excellent white oak casks much sought after by the rum producers of the Caribbean and a vital component in producing rum of enduring quality.

Australia: The Rum Rebellion

In August 1806, Captain William Bligh (1754–1817) was appointed as the fourth governor of New South Wales, Australia. Bligh, who is most famously known for being in command of HMS *Bounty*, seventeen years earlier, when the mutiny occurred and subsequently being cast adrift along with loyal members of his crew. Although the mutiny was not prompted by Bligh specifically, as mutinies were not uncommon on English ships at this time due to issues of over service and conditions, his reportedly hot temper and reputation for being a strict disciplinarian probably did not help to mitigate the situation. It was, however, these character traits that led him to be recommended for the appointment of governor of this penal colony as there was seen to be widespread corruption and he was considered to be just the man to sort it out.

For the past twenty years, the New South Wales Corps (later nicknamed The Rum Corps), comprising around 700 men, had been stationed in the colony in order to support the governor in keeping law and order. However, when the corps was established in 1789 to relieve the New South Wales Marines Corps that had accompanied the First Fleet to New South Wales, those recruited to serve were made up of officers and men who enrolled with the expectation of a better standard of living and financial reward than they could expect in England. Officers were granted land by the governor, along with free labour supplied by convicts, and allowed to engage in lucrative trading. Many of the enlisted soldiers were made up of skilled and semi-skilled men who after becoming unemployed in England due to the Industrial Revolution saw this as an opportunity to earn good wages and quick promotion.

The officers who received land endowments built comfortable homes and farms, the produce from which they sold for profit, and this led to Sydney Cove becoming a regular stop-off for trading ships because its remoteness ensured favorable commercial conditions. The colony's isolated location also meant that there was a shortage of note and coin currency so, in order to trade, an intricate barter system was developed by those in control of goods, which was mainly based on food, clothing and alcohol, the most popular of which was rum. In fact, it was not uncommon for lower-ranking soldiers as well as convicts to be paid in rum.

One of the officers to benefit substantially from this trading system, and who would become one of Bligh's main adversaries, was John Macarthur (1767–1834). After being granted land and privileges by the colony's first governor, Francis Grose, Macarthur soon became an extremely influential and wealthy man and a pioneer of Australia's wool industry. The British government was aware of the power wielded by those like Macarthur and instructed the second and third governors, John Hunter and Philip Gidley King, to put an end to the military's control of trade as well as to stamp out the widespread drunkenness being fuelled by men being remunerated with rum. Both governors were, unsurprisingly, unsuccessful due to the large amounts of money at stake in these lucrative business ventures, and so the government decided on William Bligh (nicknamed 'that Bounty bastard' by men in the fleet) in the hope that he could regulate the rum trade in the colony.

By the time Governor Bligh took up office Macarthur was a private citizen (having resigned from the army rather than face a court martial for an attack on his commanding officer) and a highly influential force in the region. Bligh and Macarthur locked horns almost immediately over a provisional land grant that led to Bligh threatening to remove Macarthur's principal holding and also accusing him of attempted manipulation of commodity prices. Bligh set about introducing reforms that tightened government control over visiting ships and their cargos and ordered that sterling should be the only payment currency. He also directed that illicit stills be destroyed and prohibited the bartering of spirits for grain, labour, or any other commodities, especially rum, which incensed both the landowners and the corps, who felt that, being a naval officer, Bligh was meddling with their military command.

The acrimony continued between the two men and culminated in Bligh taking legal proceedings against Macarthur over an incident involving one of Macarthur's trading vessels. Bligh ordered that Macarthur appear before a court, which he refused to do on the grounds that the colony's judge advocate, Richard Atkins, owed him money, and so he was arrested and bailed to go on trial on 25 January 1808.

Macarthur's impending trial did not bode well for the settlement's more affluent colonists, including the corps officers, which is likely to have had a bearing on their subsequent decision to support Macarthur's proposition to depose Bligh. The trial jury, comprising corps officers, refused to recognise the court and Bligh responded by ordering them be charged with treason. This led their commanding officer, George Johnston, to claim that the safety of the colony would be at risk if they were removed from their duties and that it was Bligh who should be removed from office for the good of all.

And so, on 26 January 1808, the 'Rum Rebellion' took place when Major George Johnson marched 400 New South Wales Corps to Government House in Sydney to detain Governor William Bligh. John Macarthur had written a petition supported by 151 colonists, most of whom had signed after Bligh's arrest, and a rebel government was subsequently formed, led by Johnston and Macarthur.

Despite being encouraged to return to England, Bligh resisted, wanting to stay until a successor had been installed by the British government, and so remained under house arrest for almost a year. Finally, in March 1809, Bligh agreed to return to England, but once aboard ship he surreptitiously sailed to Hobart to seek assistance from its lieutenant-governor, David Collins. However, Collins declined to help, and so Bligh remained on board ship for another year until he at last got news that the uprising had been declared illegal by the British Foreign Office and was officially a mutiny. This meant that a new governor, Lachlan Macquarie, had been appointed to replace him, leading Bligh to return to Sydney to gather evidence for the forthcoming court martial, in England, of the rebellion's ringleaders.

Macquarie was accompanied by the 73rd Regiment, which relieved the New South Wales Corps who returned to England where their leaders would answer the charges against them. Sensing the game was up, Johnston and Macarthur had already returned to England the previous year in order to formulate their defence and try to undermine Bligh before his return.

The outcome of the court martial was that George Johnston was found guilty and dismissed from the army – a relatively lenient punishment as he was free to return to New South Wales as a private citizen in 1813 to continue to benefit from his already prosperous business interests. John Macarthur, on the other hand, was already a civilian and faced the prospect of being returned to Sydney to face trial for treason. However, after protracted negotiations lasting until 1817, he was finally given permission to return without facing trial on the understanding that he withdrew from public affairs.

Bligh was not entirely absolved for his part in the incident but nevertheless received a backdated promotion to rear admiral and another, in 1814, to vice admiral, although he was never again given a significant command.

RUM REBELLION CARTOON

Two years after the Rum Rebellion of 1806, when soldiers of the New South Wales Corps, led by Major George Johnston, marched to Government House to detain Governor William Bligh, a watercolour cartoon was exhibited by an unknown artist that depicted Bligh being dragged from hiding under a servant's bed. The watercolour was exhibited in Sydney in 1808 and was possibly the first public art exhibition in Australia.

There is no factual evidence to suggest that Bligh had actually concealed himself under a bed to avoid detection, but as with all political cartoons the subjects are caricaturised and exaggerated. The message conveyed in the cartoon is that the New South Wales Corps officers were gentlemen and that Bligh was a coward who was not worthy of being governor, therefore justifying their cause.

This is Australia's earliest surviving political cartoon and the original is held by the State Library of New South Wales.

Inner Circle Rum Red Dot

Inner Circle Rum was first produced by CSR (The Colonial Sugar Refinery, an Australian sugar-production company) for the company's directors, the board and some *very important people* – hence the name, Inner Circle. As the making of rum was never meant to be a commercial endeavour, the aim was to produce the best rum possible and no expense was spared. The decision not to use column distillation but pot stills using molasses from Fiji and ageing in oak (generally ex-bourbon casks and new American white oak in the case of the green circle) for at least two years provides Inner Circle's delightful flavour profile.

CSR was founded in 1855 and established refineries in Australia, New Zealand and Fiji. They built the Harwood Distillery in 1873 on the Clarence river in northern New South Wales and started domestic rum production. By 1890 they opened a distillery in Fiji and in 1901 in Pyrmont, an inner-city suburb of Sydney. Using pot stills, this distillery produced the highest-quality rum, using sugar cane from both Australia and Fiji. The current Inner Circle rum is based on the distilling methods used in the early 1900s in Pyrmont. Although entered into spirit shows and winning its first gold medal at the Sydney Agricultural Show in 1950, it was kept for the exclusive consumption of the CSR Board of Directors and the inner circle of CSR management. The ritual of presenting a bottle, once a year, to their best clients created a demand that would ultimately force this product into the marketplace. Opened up to the Australian market in the early 1950s, Inner

Circle rum immediately developed a cult following. It was originally released in three strengths: Underproof, Overproof and 33 Overproof Full Strength, with a different coloured circle marking each strength. In 1986 CSR decided to sell their rum distillery interests and Inner Circle was removed from the market. A great Australian icon disappeared.

It took an exuberant yachtsman (sailors always have had a thing about rum – see Rums of Distinction: Tres Hombres) and a stubborn old distiller to revitalise the brand in 2000. Stuart Gilbert, former Olympic yachtsman and an avid fan of Inner Circle rum, made the acquaintance of Malcolm Campbell, the man responsible for the distillation of Inner Circle from 1972 to 1986. Stuart had the financial means and Malcolm still had original yeast cultures in his fridge and, of course, the original recipe. They acquired the name, purchased and re-engineered the old Beenleigh Distillery in Queensland, and Inner Circle was reborn, almost immediately winning every conceivable award around the world including the Jim Murray Trophy at the 2004 International Wines and Spirits Competition in London.

Inner Circle rum must be Australia's most awarded spirit and, tasting it, it's easy to understand why. A broad, amber rum, the iconic Inner Circle Red Dot (40 per cent ABV) rum is a great mid-range mixing rum not that far removed from Mount Gay's Eclipse but with a peaty, whisky finish. Inner circle also produce an overproof Inner Circle Green Dot marque at 57.2 per cent ABV, which is understandably sharper on the palate but, with a little watering, has a peppercorn spiciness in the finish.

Rum Running and Bootlegging During Prohibition

The Volstead Act (the legal ratification of the Eighteenth Amendment) came into effect on 17 January 1920, prohibiting the sale of alcohol in the United States and almost overnight wiped out the American drinks industry. In 1916, there were 1,300 breweries producing full-strength beer in the United States; ten years later there were none. Over the same period, the number of distilleries was cut by 85 per cent, and those that survived produced industrial alcohol for medical and manufacturing purposes. Large breweries such as Coors and Anheuser-Busch turned to making 'near beer' – beer that fell below the legally stipulated 0.5 per cent alcohol level. Budweiser, the self-proclaimed 'King of Beers', gave up brewing altogether in favour of manufacturing cartons of malted milk.

Legal production of 'near beer' used less than one-tenth the amount of malt, one-twelfth the rice and hops, and one-thirtieth of the corn used to make full-strength beer before National Prohibition, thus there was a considerable hit taken by the agricultural sector too. The 318 US wineries of 1914 had dwindled to a mere twenty-seven within five years, with those only surviving courtesy of a loophole that did not prohibit the production of unfermented grape concentrate (unsurprisingly many Americans took up home-made winemaking as a hobby).

The number of liquor wholesalers was cut by 96 per cent and the number of legal retailers by 90 per cent. From 1919 to 1929, federal tax revenues from distilled spirits dropped from $365 million to less than $13 million, and revenue from fermented liquors from $117 million to virtually nothing. Amidst all this carnage, however, the demand for rum (albeit illegally imported rum) increased markedly after decades of decline in sales and popularity. The main reason for this was not a sudden change in public drinking tastes but that rum smuggled from the Caribbean was considered a safer option than dubious home-produced moonshine.

The practice of 'rum running' was the chartering of ships from Caribbean islands laden with a cargo of liquor to ports along the east coast of America. Typically, these ships would sail towards a US port and drop anchor just outside American jurisdiction (which was 3 nautical miles offshore in 1920 but hurriedly extended to 12 miles three years later) and form a 'rum row' (a blockade of boats). Smaller boats of bootleggers would then rendezvous with the 'row', barter for prices with different ships and sneak the cargo back to land. Since rum was in plentiful and cheap supply in the Caribbean, it became one of the most commonly smuggled liquors to keep the underground speakeasies stocked.

The risks, of course, were considerable, not least because the US Navy loaned twenty destroyers to the US Coast Guard at the advent of Prohibition to intercept and deter illegal smuggling of alcohol. The need to move the cargo undetected (usually under the cover of darkness or in adverse weather) also presented risks, as did the involvement of organised crime networks. The first rum rows sprung up along the Florida coast but soon spread to New Orleans and San Francisco, with perhaps the largest and most famous being off the coast of New Jersey.

The Queen of the Bahamas: Gertrude 'Cleo' Lythgoe

One of the most colourful of the rum runners was Gertrude 'Cleo' Lythgoe (dates unknown), a contemporary of the king of rum runners, William 'Bill' McCoy (1877–1948). Lythgoe was born in Bowling Green, Ohio, towards the end of the nineteenth century (she was notoriously reticent to state her actual age) and was the youngest of ten children. It is believed her parents were Anglo–Scottish immigrants and she was orphaned at an early age after the sudden death of her mother left her father unable to look after the family. Lythgoe excelled at school and moved to New York where she worked as a stenographer. Shortly before Prohibition came into force, Lythgoe found work for a British liquor importer, most probably as a junior accounts clerk and secretary. When the bombshell of the Volstead Act landed in 1920, Lythgoe faced an uncertain future but managed to persuade her employer that there was money to be made from importing liquor from the British Bahamas.

Gertrude 'Cleo' Lythgoe relocated to Nassau where she set up a wholesale liquor export business and rented a room in the notorious Lucerne Hotel, a hotbed for smugglers, petty criminals and ex-pat dropouts. In her autobiography *The Bahama Queen* (1966) Lythgoe describes life in the Lucerne: 'All types and nationalities conversed on the front veranda waiting for the ringing of the dinner bell ... Many newspaper reporters and feature writers sat by the hour at the bar gathering rich material to be woven into fiction.'

Among Lythgoe's fellow residents at the Lucerne were champion beer drinker Big Dutch; a representative of an

English tobacco firm 'who passes directly to his room with a very important and upstage attitude'; Tony, the scion of a wealthy Philadelphia family who 'spoke seven languages but was rarely sober'; a Palm Beach society parasite known as 'The Count'; a pompous British army major; and a cowboy called Tex with a weakness for 'wine, women and song'. Perhaps fittingly, the manageress of the Lucerne at the time was an Irish American ex-nurse named Dorothy Donnelle, whose only previous employment had been in an Indiana insane asylum and was referred to by the hotel's residents as 'the mother'.

Nassau during Prohibition inevitably attracted all manner of shady characters, such were the riches to made from rum running (a barrel of premium Scotch whisky or high-grade rum could fetch an estimated 700 per cent profit on the black market in the booze-starved US). It is remarkable that a young, single woman, whose only work experience was as a typist and accounts clerk, could not only survive in such a volatile and febrile environment but become a highly successful smuggler and gain the nickname 'Queen of the Bahamas'.

Lythgoe was a strikingly beautiful woman – tall, slim, raven-haired and always immaculately dressed in the finest fashions (she gained the nickname 'Cleo' on account of her supposed resemblance to Queen Cleopatra). There is no doubt she had plenty of suitors and yet she never married, although she maintained a close friendship whilst living on Nassau with the legendary rum runner and scourge of the US authorities Bill McCoy. McCoy described Lythgoe to New York journalist Robert Wigley in the following terms:

She was a tall slender girl with black hair, a brain as steady as her own dark eyes, and a history that was nobody's business. She came to Nassau as agent for Haig and McTavish's Scotch whisky, no one knew from where. She made no secret of her background, but she told an entirely different tale to everyone who asked. She was born in California. She had been born in India. She was a gypsy. She had been raised in the Middle West. You could take your choice ... Members of the rum mob who drew their own conclusions concerning her and then tried to operate accordingly, probably will recall the breath-taking fury she could show, and one or two must remember the pistol jammed into their ribs by way of making things clear.

One legend concerning Lythgoe tells how she dealt with any attempts by other rum runners to interfere with or disrupt her successful business. Lythgoe had been tipped off that a rival sales agent had been spreading rumours to potential clients and buyers that Lythgoe traded in sub-standard and/ or counterfeit liquor. In actual fact, taking her cue from her mentor, McCoy, Lythgoe prided herself in smuggling only the finest-grade spirits and never watered any of her barrels down, as was common practice amongst rum runners. Incensed by the slander, and in a scene reminiscent of a gangster movie, Lythgoe tracked the culprit down to a nearby barbers, marched into the shop, stuck a gun to the startled man's forehead and told him to leave Nassau because if she ever saw him again she'd pull the trigger.

Although Lythgoe mainly acted as a 'middle man' between liquor producers and rum runners, organising prices and supervising shipments, she was not averse to getting her hands dirty in the murky world of smuggling. On several occasions she made trips aboard McCoy's schooner to the rum row off the New Jersey coast to oversee the sale of her consignments and earning an estimated $100,000 per trip.

Stories of the beautiful, gun-toting, female smuggler operating out of the Bahamas began appearing in US newspapers and earned Lythgoe celebrity status. Unfortunately, this also drew her business activities to the attention of the US authorities. In 1922 the US government, aware of the activities of the Nassau rum runners, had filed an official complaint to the British Colonial Office that the blind eye being turned towards smuggling in the British colonies was undermining US Law. The Secretary of State for the Colonies at the time was a certain Sir Winston Churchill (1874–1965) who point-blank refused to take any action or intervene, stating his belief that Prohibition was 'an affront to the history of mankind'.

Nonetheless, in 1924 Lythgoe was arrested on Nassau by federal agents, transported back to New Orleans and charged with smuggling 1,000 barrels of whisky and rum into the city. Although Lythgoe had arranged the consignment, she had entrusted its delivery to a third party who had attempted to double-cross her and sell the liquor for his own profit and was subsequently apprehended by the US Coast Guard. Lythgoe was able to demonstrate that she was travelling elsewhere at the time of the alleged incident and the case was thrown out of court, leaving her free to return to Nassau.

In April 1924, the US government successfully petitioned to have its jurisdiction to the waters around its coastlines increased from 3 miles to 12 miles. This meant that rum rows now had to drop anchor further from land in open international waters, which made rum-running operations considerably more difficult and hazardous. These added complications plus her experiences in custody in New Orleans led Lythgoe to decide to quit whilst she was ahead and retire. In her memoirs she writes of encountering a feeling that a 'jinx' was following her that would lead ultimately to her death. When interviewed by long-time admirer Robert Wigley for an article in the *New York Times* in 1926, Lythgoe said, 'I just beat my jinx before it got me ... I saw the signs when I was taking some whiskey from Nassau to another British island.'

Quite what these signs were – possibly a skirmish with another rum runner who often boarded rival boats to steal cargo – is unclear. Whatever the reason, Lythgoe retired and moved back to the US, where she settled first in Miami and then Detroit (where she set up a lucrative car-hire business) before seeing out her final years writing her memoirs in Los Angeles, where she died in 1974 at the estimated age of 86. As Wigley wrote of her when first encountering Lythgoe in the early 1920s, 'She stands alone and fearless – a woman who would grace any London drawing room ... she has commanded the respect and homage of this motley and dubious throng, [and] is known in the trade as "the Queen of the Bahamas".' As news of her passing reached Nassau, the British flags at the port were lowered to half-mast for several days as a mark of respect for their former smuggler 'queen'.

The Rise and Mysterious Disappearance of 'Spanish Marie'

As one feisty female smuggler settled down to enjoy an easier life, another rose to prominence to take up the mantle of queen of the bootleggers. Marie 'Spanish Marie' Waite inherited a rum-running business when her husband, Florida gangster Charlie Waite, was killed in a shootout with the US Coast Guard at Biscayne Bay in 1926. It is uncertain if Marie had had any involvement in her husband's nefarious activities up until that point, or if she was merely driven by a desire to avenge his death, but she certainly took over Charlie Waite's criminal network with some aplomb.

Waite was the product of a Swedish father and Mexican mother – genes that furnished her 6ft-plus stature, olive skin, flowing black hair and piercing blue eyes. In his book *Rum War at Sea* (2001), historian Malcolm Willoughby describes Waite as 'a fickle and dangerous person, with morals as free as the four winds'. Stories and rumours of Waite paint her as a classic femme fatale, playing on her stunning good looks

to satisfy her greed and ambition. Various accounts have her disposing of a litany of lovers by encasing them in 'concrete boots' and dropping them overboard or seducing local law-enforcement officers in Key West with her money and charms. Although many of these tales about Waite remain uncorroborated, bribery and blackmail were common tactics of organised crime networks during and post Prohibition, so it is safe to assume that the smuggler who became known as 'Spanish Marie' was indeed a thoroughly bad egg.

Beyond her notoriety for ruthlessness, however, it is easy to overlook that Waite was also a very shrewd businesswoman and an ingenious smuggler. Waite set up business in Havana, Cuba, with the express intention of importing a plentiful supply of Cuban rum. Cuba had come late to the sugar and rum party, mainly due to early Spanish indolence, but by the late nineteenth century there were more than 1,300 rum distilleries on the island (see The Rise of Cuba). Prohibition was a godsend for the Cuban economy, both in terms of producing and exporting rum, and a huge hike in the number of American tourists. Pan Am airlines joined forces with Bacardi to run an aggressive advertising campaign to entice Americans to the bars and beaches of Cuba with slogans such as 'Fly to Paradise and Leave the Dry Lands Behind'. Up until Prohibition there had been a considerable market for Cuban rum in the US, largely due to the 'cocktail craze', and it was this plus the close geographical proximity of the island to the Florida coast (100 miles) that Waite ruthlessly exploited.

'Spanish Marie' invested in a flotilla of fifteen schooners, sloops and small motor boats, all of which were fast and versatile boats capable of outrunning the US Coast Guard.

Typically, Waite would send a convoy of four large schooners from Havana, three laden to the brim with cheap liquor and one with the firepower to protect the cargo and act as an 'enforcer'. If detected by the Coast Guard, the 'enforcer' would engage them in an exchange of fire long enough for the three fast cargo ships to make an escape. Once inside US waters, the cargo ships would then rendezvous with the motorboats who swiftly ferried the barrels of liquor to the mainland. Waite's operations proved remarkably successful, and such was her skill in evading the authorities that within a couple of years 'Spanish Marie' and her cohorts were the principal rum runners along the Florida coast from Palm Beach to Key West.

Gradually the penny dropped and the US Coast Guard invested in faster boats equipped with more sophisticated communications equipment to enable them to coordinate patrols more effectively and set traps for the smugglers. Waite responded to this sudden shift in advantage towards the authorities by equipping her boats with radio equipment and setting up a pirate (no pun intended) radio-transmitting station in Key West. The radio station on land communicated intelligence on Coast Guard operations and instructions to the boats offshore via an elaborate code of seemingly innocent Spanish words and phrases.

Eventually, however, the Coast Guard deciphered the code and laid a trap for Waite at Coconut Grove, Miami. On 12 March 1928, Waite was apprehended unloading a consignment of rum from Bimini from her flagship *Kid Boots*. The authorities had tricked Waite into believing the coast was clear via a fake radio transmission and, having worked out the boat's landing destination, they were lying in wait for her when she arrived. Waite it seemed had been so convinced that the consignment would arrive undetected that she left her two small children at home unattended – an oversight she quickly turned to her advantage. Under interrogation Waite broke down and delivered an Oscar-winning performance of the distraught and distressed mother, pleading with her captors to grant her a bail bond so she could tend to her abandoned children. Remarkably the authorities fell for the ploy and posted a $500 bond for Waite's temporary release on condition she attend a preliminary trial hearing hurriedly arranged for the following day.

Waite failed to attend the hearing in person but sent an attorney who claimed she was suffering from a nervous breakdown. The court extended the bond to $3,000 on condition of a medical report being submitted to verify Waite's condition. Waite never appeared in court and absconded along with her boats and any trace of her smuggling operation. At the time of her disappearance it is estimated she had amassed a personal fortune of close to US$1 million – more than enough money to disappear and never be found. Inevitably, rumours and conspiracy theories circulated as to 'Spanish Marie's' whereabouts and fate, ranging from living under an assumed name as a plantation owner in Cuba, to having been abducted and killed by a rival crime syndicate. The truth of the circumstances of her sudden disappearance will probably never be known other than Waite used all of her feminine wiles and considerable cunning to evade the authorities one final time.

BAD BITCH SPANISH MARIE

In 2012 two local chefs and entrepreneurs opened an artisan, small-batch rum distillery in Key West, Florida—the first legally licensed distillery in the island city. Naturally enough, the name given to their signature rum, which was distilled, filtered and aged on the premises, was a tribute to Key West's most famous rum runner, Marie Waite.

Key West Legal Rum's Bad Bitch Spanish Marie is a dark rum aged in vintage French oak barrels previously used to age red wine and brandy. The barrels are also cured with salt before ageing, adding hints of tannin and salted caramel. Although weighing in at a normally hefty 40 per cent ABV, Bad Bitch Spanish Marie is surprisingly smooth due to the six-time small-batch distilling copper-pot processes. By way of added historical veracity, it is thought that Marie Waite's tipple of choice was a rum punch made with red wine.

The Bootleggers Behind Captain Morgan Rum

The Captain Morgan brand of rum is the second largest rum brand in the world (second only to Bacardi), and although the Captain Morgan brand likes to portray itself as a 'heritage' brand, it was actually the work of product developers at former multinational drinks corporation Seagram. Captain Morgan rum was launched by Seagram in the 1940s and, playing mercilessly on Hollywood's obsession with pirates and skulduggery, quickly established for itself a place in the rum market despite it being a fairly mediocre blend. The Captain was an advertising exec's dream and the fact that it took its name from a real-life pirate/privateer (see The Real Pirates of the Caribbean) gave the brand added kudos. Ironically, the origins of Seagram and the business activities of its founders, the Bronfman family, are arguably as opportunistic and morally murky as any of the antics of Sir Henry Morgan 200 years before.

Samuel Bronfman and his two brothers Harry and Abe were first-generation Russian–Jewish immigrants whose father, Yechiel, had been a successful tobacco farmer in Moldova. The Bronfman family fled Imperial Russia in 1889 to escape the anti-Semitic Tsarist regime of Alexander III and settled in Canada. After an initial period of hardship working on the construction of the Northern Canadian Railway, Yechiel started a number of small businesses, including a firewood delivery firm and a horse-trading network. In 1903 the Bronfman family borrowed money to buy the Anglo-American Hotel in Emerton, Manitoba. Over the next decade the Bronfmans' business grew to the extent that they bought up and developed several hotels in Manitoba and spread their business interests to other Canadian provinces such as Ontario and Saskatchewan.

Although often dogged by anti-Semitic suspicion from local authorities and rumours that, despite their outwardly respectable appearances, their hotels were little more than fronts for illegal gambling and prostitution dens, Samuel Bronfman and his two brothers continued to prosper. In 1916 the temperance movement that had been spreading across Canada reached Manitoba and Ontario, spelling disaster for the Bronfmans' business interests. Samuel Bronfman, realising that the sale of alcohol was by far the most lucrative aspect of the business, started producing and distributing cheap whisky and rum. Although the sale of hard liquor was prohibited in Manitoba and Ontario, it was not illegal to 'import' liquor from province to province. The Bronfmans skilfully took advantage of this legal loophole by setting up mail-order companies in different province and literally selling their own products to themselves for sale in their various establishments and to 'private' customers.

By 1918 most Canadian provinces had adopted prohibition laws and begun to tighten regulation of the movement of alcohol between provinces. Despite new laws causing the closure of the Bronfmans' mail-order scams, Harry discovered that the sale of alcohol was still permitted in the province of Saskatchewan for medicinal purposes. This proved a watershed moment in the brothers' career as they promptly filed for and received a licence to create a wholesale drug company, which they named the Canada Pure Drug Corporation (CPDC). Although the CPDC provided small quantities of medicinal alcohol to pharmacies and hospitals, its main activities were confined to importing vast quantities of contraband whisky, which were re-bottled and sold on the black market. By the time Prohibition started in the US in 1920, the Bronfman brothers had stockpiled huge warehouses full of illegal liquor along the border between Saskatchewan and North Dakota, which provided perfect access to the American market. Not content with the huge turnover from their import and export business, the brothers' next move was to start their own distillery business to produce and bottle their own stock.

Not surprisingly, the Bronfmans' position at the forefront of the underground liquor business began to attract the unwanted attentions both of federal enforcement agencies in Canada and organised crime organisations in the US. Indeed, 1922 proved to be something of an *annus horribilis* for the Bronfmans as they were indicted for non-payment of income tax by the Department of National Revenue after it discovered that it hadn't received a tax return from the family for over five years. Then, at the height of a crime wave surrounding bootlegging and rum running, Paul Matoff, a family member, was murdered outside one of the Bronfmans' warehouses close to the US border. Matoff's killers were never found and various theories exist as to the circumstances behind the crime, from bungled robbery to gangland hit. The ensuing public outcry that the case provoked was enough for the local authorities to effectively ban the brothers from continuing with their export activities.

Samuel Bronfman moved to Montreal and set up a new distillery business. Quebec was one of the few Canadian provinces to have resisted prohibition laws (province prohibition lasted less than a year before being repealed due to intense public pressure) and provided the ideal environment in which to try to legitimise the family business. After a couple of years' consolidation, Samuel Bronfman purchased what would become the famous Joseph E. Seagram Distillery in Waterloo, Ontario, and began to plan carefully for the end of Prohibition in the US.

When the end finally came, however, the Bronfmans again found themselves under investigation for various federal offences relating to tax evasion, company fraud and false accounting. After a protracted and complicated legal battle, the brothers were acquitted but were hit with a $3 million bill from the US Treasury Department for unpaid customs and excise tariffs.

As the Seagram brands began to corner a significant slice of the US liquor market, the Bronfmans embarked on an assiduous public-relations drive to obscure their Prohibition-era misdemeanours. Samuel Bronfman began setting up various charitable foundations and became a major figure in the Canadian Jewish Congress, which provided consider-able support for Jewish refugees and Holocaust survivors after the Second World War. In 1967, Samuel Bronfman was made a Companion of the Order of Canada – the highest rank in the Canadian honours system awarded to individuals for their humanity, philanthropy and services to the nation. By his death in 1971, the mythology of the powerful but benign immigrant family made good was well established. It is only fitting then that the Bronfmans' spectacular rise in the first half of the twentieth century should be mirrored by a sudden and ignominious decline at its close.

Seagram continued to prosper throughout the 1970s and '80s, at one point owning a portfolio of over 250 brands. Under the chairmanship of Edgar Bronfman, the com-pany started an aggressive expansion programme into areas other than liquor production and distribution. This, in hindsight, proved to be the start of the downfall of the Bronfman dynasty. After becoming involved in a protracted bidding war for the oil company Conoco, Seagram became saddled with considerable debts. Edgar Bronfman took over as chief executive and began to indulge his passion for the entertainment business by buying up controlling interests in Universal Studios and music companies MCA and Polygram in 1995. These investments proved to be disastrous for Seagram and within five years the entertainment operations were acquired by French media conglomerate Vivendi and the once-famous drinks company was auctioned off to various bidders such as Coca-Cola and Pernod Ricard. After making their fortune with shrewd manipulation of market forces, it is ironic that the Bronfman empire should disintegrate when those same forces turned against it.

In 2001, drinks giant Diageo purchased the Captain Morgan brand from Seagram, rebranding the name as Captain Morgan's Spiced. Although Captain Morgan was originally produced and blended by the Long Pond distillery, which Samuel Bronfman purchased from the Jamaican government in the 1940s, Seagram moved production of Captain Morgan to distilleries in Puerto Rico in the 1950s. In 2008, Diageo announced that they were relocating production of Captain Morgan to Saint Croix in the US Virgin Islands – a controversial move that caused consternation in Puerto Rico and led to questions being raised about corporate tax evasion in the US Senate. One recent innovation by Diageo that has proved effective is changing the company's advertising tagline to 'Live Life like the Captain' from the frankly snigger-worthy slogan of the Seagram era, 'Everyone Needs a Little Captain in Them'.

PART 4

THE RISE OF CUBA

HAVANA CLUB VERSUS BACARDI IN
THE RUM FIGHT OF THE CENTURY

Although Columbus claimed Cuba for the Spanish Crown on his second voyage in 1494 and the Spanish set up permanent settlements on the island in the early decades of the sixteenth century, Cuba retained the status of a half-forgotten cousin of the Spanish Americas for over 200 years. The reasons for this can probably be attributed to the Spanish obsession with South American gold and silver as they weren't much better at developing or protecting their other interests in the Caribbean either. Nonetheless, Cuba was of considerable strategic importance because of its location and is the largest island in the Caribbean, which makes it all the more curious why Cuba spent so long as a sleeping giant.

Granted, the Spanish did establish tentative plantations of sugar and tobacco as Cuba's primary products (and they remain so to this day) and the island soon supplanted Hispaniola as the prime Spanish base in the Caribbean. However, in order for the plantations to expand and develop, an increase in the labour force was needed, especially as the indigenous Taíno population had been all but wiped out by the middle of the sixteenth century.

Imported African slaves took up some of the slack, although Spain again seemed curiously reticent to embrace the transatlantic slave trade with quite the same gusto as their British, Dutch and French Caribbean counterparts. The imposition of restrictive Spanish trade laws, coupled with the effects of the often-volatile relations between the European superpowers, made it difficult for Cuban colonists to keep apace with the seventeenth- and eighteenth-century advances in processing sugar cane pioneered in British Barbados and French St-Domingue (Haiti).

The advent of the Seven Years War in 1756, causing conflict across three continents, eventually spilled over into the Caribbean islands. As Spain was allied with France this put them in the firing line of their old foe the British. In 1762 a fleet of British warships carrying 4,000 troops under the command of George Keppel (1724–1772) set out from the south coast of England on an expedition to capture Cuba. Previous attempts by Britain, most notably in 1741 and 1748, had ultimately proved unsuccessful, partly due to poor planning and on one occasion a yellow-fever epidemic. The British fleet arrived at the coast of Cuba on 6 June and, despite meeting some spirited resistance from the Spanish, had Havana besieged within two months. On 14 August the Spanish finally surrendered, and Keppel and his men entered Havana, with the commander installing himself as governor of the island. The British only occupied Cuba for little over a year before it was bargained away in the Treaty of Paris in 1763 in exchange for Florida. Nonetheless, the opening up of previously shuttered trade routes brought in new goods and products that had previously been in short supply. The British occupiers, clearly initially planning for a long stay, radically expanded the island's sugar plantations and imported 4,000 slaves from West Africa as a labour force – this number of slaves amounted to approximately 10 per cent of the total number of slaves Spain had shipped to Cuba in the previous 250 years.

The Haitian revolution – a general term for a series of insurrections on French St-Domingue that took place between 1791 and 1803 – also played a key part in Cuba's renaissance. Thousands of French colonial refugees flooded into Cuba, fleeing the slave rebellions on St-Domingue, and brought with them slaves and their expertise in sugar refining and coffee growing in the 1790s and early nineteenth century. Cuba was perfectly equipped for growing sugar due to its size and climate, with its rich soil resources and sufficient rainfall. The new technological advances paved the way for a much more effective and efficient means of producing sugar. The planters harnessed natural resources to drive water mills, built enclosed furnaces and utilised steam engines to produce higher-quality sugar on an industrial level that soon outstripped other colonies in the Caribbean, where the soil had become tired and less fertile from centuries of aggressive planting. Hand in hand with the massive boom in Cuban sugar production in the nineteenth century came flourishing rum distilleries. After all, they had to do something with all the molasses. By the mid 1860s there were more than 1,300 rum distilleries in Cuba producing and exporting 20 million litres a year.

Despite the successes of the sugar and rum industries in the nineteenth century, Cuba regularly found itself in the throes of political upheaval. As noted above, Spain hadn't been early adopters of the West African slave trade but more than made up for lost time during the nineteenth century, when they doggedly resisted international pressure for abolitionism. Officially, the slave trade was outlawed under a treaty with the British as early as 1820 and yet Spanish plantation owners on Cuba continued to turn a blind eye to the ban up until the middle of the nineteenth century. Lax enforcement of the slave-trade ban had resulted in a dramatic 'illegal' increase in imports of Africans, estimated at 90,000 slaves from 1856 to 1860. This occurred in the face of a strong abolitionist movement on the island, and rising costs among the slave-holding planters in the east of Cuba. Developments in technology and farming techniques had made large numbers of slaves unnecessary and prohibitively expensive. This inevitably led to growing tensions and unrest between the growing migrant communities, the wealthy Spanish plantation owners and the Spanish government. Between 1868 and 1898 there were no fewer than three attempts to declare independence for Cuba in the form of armed insurrections against the Spanish state (known as the Ten Years War (1868–1878); the Little War (1879–1880); and the Cuban War of Independence (1895–1898). America had been hungrily eyeing a possible annexation of Cuba for several decades and it was American support that finally tipped the balance in the Cubans' favour. Arguably, however, the aggressive American interventions into Cuban business and commerce over the early decades of the twentieth century merely meant that Cuba had traded one imperial master for another.

Havana Club versus Bacardi

Havana Club is one of the most prestigious rum brands in the world and considered by the Cuban government to be one of the country's 'Crown jewels'. The story of the brand is complex and heartbreaking, encompassing a revolution, court-room battles and a protracted slugfest between two of the largest drinks multinationals in the world.

Once upon a time there were two prominent rum-producing families in Cuba, the Bacardi family and the Arechabala family. Catalan-born Facundo Bacardi (1814–1886) emigrated from Sitges, Spain, along with his two brothers in the early 1840s and set up a general store in Santiago de Cuba. Facundo and his two brothers prospered at first, but their business fell foul of an earthquake in 1852, which was followed by a catastrophic cholera epidemic that claimed the lives of several family members and forced the family to flee back to Catalonia.

On returning to Cuba in 1855, Bacardi found that his business had been appropriated by looters and he was penniless and bankrupt. Legend has it that at this point salvation came upon a chance meeting with José Léon Boutellier, a French Cuban and descendant of a Haitian sugar dynasty. Under Boutellier's guidance, Bacardi began experimenting with distilling rum and after a few near misses hit upon a smooth, clear blend, which they charcoal filtered and aged in white oak barrels. Bacardi was a shrewd businessman and an early adopter of 'brand development', and when he and Boutellier acquired a rundown distillery in 1862, he set about 'designing' the brand – including the distinctive bat-shaped trademark that prevails on all Bacardi products to this day.

Jose Arechabala and family founded a sugar refinery and associated distillery in Cárdenas, Cuba, in 1878. For many decades the production of rum was secondary to the refinery in terms of importance to the company, but the boom in tourism from the US, particularly during the Prohibition era, (plus a decline in the price of sugar) led the company to switch attention to developing their off-shoot rum business. In 1934, just as Prohibition was lifted, the Arechabala family launched the now iconic and world-famous Havana Club brand, which rapidly established itself as a market leader in Cuban rums. Such was

Havana Club's success that the Arechabalas purchased and renovated the Palacio de los Condes de Casa Bayona (Palace of the Counts of House Bayona) – one of the oldest buildings and relics of the Spanish imperial age – which became the company's headquarters. This public show of ostentatiousness said much about the Arechabalas' growing confidence and a determination not to be cowed by the Bacardi family. The Bacardi family had commissioned the architects Esteban Rodríguez Castells and Rafael Fernández Ruenes to build an art deco office block in the centre of Havana in 1930, the majestic Edificio Bacardi – the largest building in Havana at the time. Both companies continued to prosper and expand, enjoying a virtual duopoly on Cuban rum exports to the US up until the Cuban Revolution in 1959.

The destinies of Cuba's two rum-producing dynasties diverged after Castro seized power. The Bacardi family, sensing storm clouds gathering, had relocated sizeable parts of their business to Puerto Rico and Mexico in the 1930s and '40s. Ironically, the Bacardi family had initially supported Castro's insurgents by donating money to the rebels and hanging

banners from their headquarters in Havana. However, in the aftermath of the revolution this support quickly evaporated as Castro's programme of wholesale nationalisation of Cuban businesses took hold. In October 1960, Castro seized Bacardi's assets and properties without compensation, forcing the Bacardi family into exile on Bermuda and the Bahamas. As the company already had production facilities outside of Cuba, they were able to survive and register their trademarks and brands in the US.

The Arechabala family were not so fortunate when Castro's men seized control of Havana Club's assets and forced the family into exile in the United States. On arrival in America, the Arechabalas initially intended to set up business again and held several meetings with drinks companies interested in purchasing the Havana Club trademark (including executives from their former rivals Bacardi) but failed to find any backers. Meanwhile, the Cuban government had continued producing Havana Club under the newly nationalised company of Cuba Ron, although mostly for domestic consumption and export to the Soviet Union.

Unable to restart their business, the Arechabalas' ownership of the Havana Club trademark expired in 1974 and was immediately snapped up by the Cuban government and registered in the United States. However, due to trade embargoes, the brand couldn't be sold or imported into America. In 1993 the Cuban government entered into a business partnership with drinks giant Pernod Ricard with the intention of expanding the marketing of Havana Club around the world. In desperation, and rightfully feeling betrayed, the Arechabalas sold their remaining rights to the Havana Club brand to Bacardi in 1994.

THE LEGEND OF THE GIRALDILLA: CUBAN ICON

The *Giraldilla* is one of the most symbolic and ancient icons of Havana City and also the image that adorns the label of Havana Club rum, which has itself been involved as part of the ongoing trademark dispute with Bacardi. A legend of love, history and art are all encapsulated in this little statue, created by the Cuban sculptor Gerónimo Martín Pinzón in the 1630s.

The King of Spain dispatched Spain's seventh governor, Don Hernando (or Fernando) de Soto to Cuba, on 20 March 1537 with orders to prepare an expedition to Florida as Cuba was in close proximity to the Florida Peninsula previously discovered by Juan Ponce de León.

On 12 May 1539, Hernando de Soto embarked for Florida from Havana's Harbour, known at the time as Cardenas' Harbour – a meeting point for all Spanish ships in the New World (making it a target for corsairs and pirates of the Caribbean). His expedition comprised nine vessels and 537 horses, selected from the finest in Cuba.

De Soto had ordered that his wife, Isabel de Bobadilla, should be in charge of the country whilst he was away, but it is told that Isabel spent hours on the turrets of the castle watching and waiting for the ship that would bring her husband back to her. De Soto never did come back. He had died on the banks of the Mississippi river on 30 June 1540, with his beloved wife still awaiting his return.

According to legend, it was the great passion of Isabel for Hernando that inspired the sculptor, Martín Pinzón, to make the bronze statue *Giraldilla*, which was located on the highest point on the north-west side of the Castillo de la Real Fuerza on the orders of the governor, Juan de Bitrián y Viamonte, between 1630 and 1634.

The *Giraldilla* is a weather vane in the shape of a Taíno woman who has a palm tree trunk in her right hand and the Calatrava cross in a flagpole in her left hand, her skirt raised on her right thigh. The statue is 110cm tall and has a medallion with the artist's name on her chest.

The weather vane withstood the force of tropical hurricanes until 20 October 1926, when she was finally wrested from her pedestal and thrown to the ground.

A replica now stands on the Real Fuerza and the original is safely housed in the Havana City Museum, the former Palacio de Los Capitanes Generales.

Call in the Lawyers

Bacardi, believing they had legitimate rights to the brand name, began producing a version of Havana Club in Puerto Rico for sale in the lucrative US market. This immediately drew litigation from Pernod Ricard who successfully sued Bacardi, forcing the company to halt production and sales of its version of the rum.

Bacardi responded by heavily lobbying the US Congress and in 1998 won a notable victory when the government passed the 'Bacardi Act', which protected trademarks related to expropriated Cuban companies. The argument centred on the Cuban government's original seizure of Havana Club from the Arechabalas and ruled that as such it was not legally recognised in the US. However, in 2002 the act was ruled illegal by the World Trade Organisation who accused the US government of aggressively victimising Cuba as the act did not stipulate or apply the same trademark protections to other countries in similar circumstances.

Pernod Ricard then launched a counter-offensive through the US federal courts and Trade Mark Trial and Appeal Court, focusing attention this time on the legitimacy of Bacardi producing a product under the name of Havana Club, which isn't produced in Cuba. This further round of litigation again resulted in a victory of sorts for Bacardi, who were allowed to retain the trademark in the US but required to state on bottle labels that the rum was produced in Puerto Rico. Pernod Ricard responded by registering a new trademark 'Havanista' (with a label and logo strikingly similar to the classic Havana Club design) with the intention of marketing their drink under this mark in the US if and when the Cuba–US trade embargo is lifted.

In 2016 there was a further twist in a complicated legal battle that has raged in US courts and government circles for over two decades, due to a thawing in US–Cuban relations. The lifting of trade and travel restrictions with Cuba by President Obama effectively meant that it was no longer illegal to bring Cuban-made products into the US for personal consumption (it is, however, still illegal to import Cuban goods for trading purposes). The thaw resulted in an upsurge in sales for Ron Cuba/Pernod Ricard's Havana Club, which in turn prompted the US courts to renew the Havana Club trademark registration.

Bacardi responded by filing a Freedom of Information Act request with the US Department of the Treasury asking for all documents and communications from the patent office, the Office of Foreign Assets Control, the State Department, the White House, the National Security Council, the Treasury and/or any third parties that could shed light on the sudden decision to renew the Havana Club registration.

Bacardi's senior vice president Eduardo Sánchez released a statement to the press stating that:

> We are filing this Freedom of Information Act request because the American people have the right to know the truth of how and why this unprecedented, sudden and silent action was taken by the United States government to reverse long-standing U.S. and international public policy and law that protects against the recognition or acceptance of confiscations of foreign governments.

The litigation and tit-for-tat suit and counter-suit trading in the courts remains unresolved with much depending on future relations between the United States and Cuba. Meanwhile Cuban-produced Havana Club continues to sell well across the world and is the fifth-largest-selling brand with markets particularly strong in Europe and India.

Havana Club Maximo Extra Añejo

Havana Club Maximo Extra Añejo is the ultimate rum of distinction and not one likely to be found on the bar shelves of any Havana rum shack. Handcrafted by a team of blenders under the guidance of Cuba's leading *Maestro Ronero* (master blender), Don José Navarro, Maximo Extra Añejo is considered by rum connoisseurs to be one of the finest rums ever produced. Don Navarro and his team have access to the oldest aged rums in the Havana Club cellars (some up to fifty years aged) and have expertly blended them to produce a robust yet silky smooth high-grade rum with an oaky smokiness and hints of dried fruit, dark chocolate and vanilla.

Produced in a limited edition of only 1,000 units per year, the rum is presented in an elegant hand-blown crystal decanter inspired by the decorative arts of Cuba. The *Giraldilla*, a symbol representing the city of Havana (see The Legend of the *Giraldilla*: Cuban Icon) and the trademark logo of Havana Club, is etched on to the crystal glass stopper. Each crystal decanter is individually numbered, bearing the signature of master glassmaker Paul Miller and comes in a lined wooden case with certification of origin. Although difficult to find and generally snapped up very quickly by collectors, the rum can be purchased from high-end spirits dealers for an eye-watering £1,200 a bottle. At that kind of price, it would be heresy to use it in a mojito.

PART 5

RUM AND THE ROYAL NAVY

The Traditions of the Rum 'Tot' and the Royal Navy

Navy Rum and the Rum Ration

The 'Great Rum Debate' took place in the House of Commons on 28 January 1970 as to whether rum rations should be abolished in the British Navy and the decision was made to finally scrap the long-standing tradition:

> While recognising the historical significance and service traditions associated with the tot, the rationale for the spirit issue as a compensation for poor food and living conditions no longer applies in today's navy ... And the daily issue of strong spirit is simply not appropriate in a high technology service which places emphasis on individual responsibility.
>
> – Chief of Naval Staff, Somerford Teagle, 1970

The custom of supplying sailors with rum stems back to the time when voyages became longer and drinking water, stowed on board ship, along with beer, developed algae and became slimy and unpalatable after a couple of weeks at sea. Prior to that, sailors in the British Navy had been supplied with a generous ration of 1 gallon of beer per day, which sounds a lot, but alcohol was seen to be a remedy to soften the harshness of the conditions under which they lived for long periods of time.

At some point around the middle of the seventeenth century, when expeditions to the Caribbean by British ships became frequent, sailors got their first taste of rum and, following Britain's conquest of Jamaica in 1655, it steadily started to replace beer and brandy as part of the sailor's daily rations. At this time there was no standardisation of regulations in the Royal Navy and each vessel acted independently, so the rum ration probably varied according to the discretion of the ship's commanding officer. There is some evidence that around this time rations of alcohol would be increased prior to a naval engagement in order to embolden the crew.

It was not until 1731 that the first naval regulations were recorded in 'Relating to His Majesty's Service at Sea', which included rum as part of a sailor's daily rations, showing its initial consumption in the Caribbean had spread to all sections of the navy. These regulations stated that a gallon of beer corresponded to 'a pint of wine or half a pint of brandy, rum or arrack'. In effect, sailors were consuming the equivalent of ten double shots of spirit per day, along with the prospect of sometimes being issued with extra for outstanding service or valour.

The term 'proof' in relation to the potency of alcohol was derived from the methods adopted in order to test the strength of the alcohol being procured in order to ensure that the navy was not being sold watered down rum by local suppliers. A test was devised that entailed a small quantity of gunpowder being mixed with the rum and heated on an open flame. According to the intensity at which it burned, an expert eye could judge the strength of the rum. The rum was either strong or it was not, and if it was then it had passed the 'proof' test. In actual fact, rum that burned like dry gunpowder was 57 per cent alcohol by volume and that which burned hotter or brighter was deemed to be 'overproof'. The Royal Navy prescribed 'overproof' rum in its 1731 regulations and this continued until its amendment, in 1866, to 4.5 underproof spirit.

Unsurprisingly, drunkenness amongst naval crews was rife and harsh punishments were handed down in order to try to maintain discipline aboard ships. This, combined with poor diet and disease, made the life of the average sailor pretty miserable. Scurvy, caused by vitamin C deficiency, affected crews who undertook long sea voyages, with alcohol being the main source of liquid intake when water ran out, and more men actually died of disease, malnutrition and poor hygiene than of injuries inflicted in battles.

Despite the fact that the connection between lack of vitamin C and scurvy had been well known by seamen for years, the Admiralty did not introduce lemon juice and sugar as a regular part of the naval diet until 1795. However, the complaint was less of a problem for units operating around the Caribbean islands where there was no shortage of fresh fruit on offer, and when Spain and France joined forces against the British, which led to oranges and lemons becoming scarce, they were substituted with Caribbean limes, which led to the British being nicknamed 'limeys'.

One man, who cared very much about the welfare of his men was Admiral Edward Vernon (1684–1757). Vernon was well respected by his men for his outstanding tactical skills in battle as well as his concern for their well-being, and he earned the nickname of 'Old Grog' after the heavy grogram cloak made from a mixture of silk, mohair and wool that he always wore. Vernon was concerned about the amount of alcohol his crew consumed and so, on 21 August 1740, he issued Captain's Order No.349, which directed that the provision of rum should be mixed with water and suggested that 'good husbandmen may from the saving of their salt provisions and bread, purchase sugar and limes to make it more palatable to them'. He also stated that the Lieutenant of the Watch should oversee the diluting of the rum and it should be served twice a day, and the ship's purser should call 'up spirits' before delivering the men their ration. From that time on the diluted rum was known as grog. The daily issue of half a pint of rum was to be mixed with 1 quart of water and issued twice a day, before noon and after at the end of the working day. The practice became widespread but was not officially introduced into navy regulations until 1756.

Due to habitual drunkenness and associated disciplinary problems aboard ship, in 1824 the British Navy decided to cut the rum ration by half, to one-quarter of a pint per day. This would obviously not have gone down well with the sailors so, to placate them, they were duly compensated with a pay increase, plus additional rations of meat, tea and cocoa.

The serving of grog twice a day soon spread beyond the British Navy. Robert Smith (1757–1842), the second United States Secretary of the Navy (from 1801 to 1809) substituted American rye whiskey for imported rum as the American sailors preferred it and nicknamed it 'Bob Smith' rather than grog. However, the ration of 'Bob Smith' was fairly short-lived as American shipowners banned merchant seamen from consuming spirits in 1848 for insurance purposes and reasons of efficiency, and the American Navy followed suit in September 1862.

British society's attitude towards alcohol consumption started to change, influenced by the rise of the temperance movements in the late nineteenth century, although the Admiralty had, again, been discussing the levels of spirit drinking and its consequential effect on performance as early as 1850, when the Admiralty's 'Grog Committee' released a report recommending that the ration be abolished. After much debate, the navy decided that, rather than do away with it altogether, the ration would be halved again to one-eighth of a pint of rum per day.

And so, the eighth of a pint of rum remained the standard issue until grog was discontinued in 1970. Gradually, the serving of the grog had become a daily ceremonial event. The boatswain's mate would pipe 'Up Spirits', which was the signal for the petty officer to retrieve the keys to the spirit room and, in procession along with the ship's cooper and a group of Royal Marines, they would watch over the filling of a keg with a one-eighth of a pint of rum for every rating and petty officer on board who was aged over 20 (with the exception of anyone under punishment). The keg was then carried to the deck by two marines who stood guard. Cooks from the petty officers' mess then held out jugs for the sergeant of the marines to dispense the ration, overseen by the chief steward who stated the number of men who would be drinking in each petty officers' mess. When that was done, the rum was mixed in a cask with two parts water to become grog to be given to the ratings.

The crew were called at noon by the boatswain's mate piping 'Muster for Rum', and the cooks from each mess lined up carrying tin buckets for the sergeant of marines to ladle out the authorised number of tots, watched over by the petty officer of the day. Any grog left over was poured into the scuppers (drains), which ran into the sea. Petty officers had the privilege of being able to take their rum neat and so were served first, followed by the diluted grog for the ratings. Up until the early twentieth century, rum diluted with water at a 6:1 ratio (six parts water to one part grog) was issued as a punishment for those sailors who had been found guilty of drunkenness.

The United States Navy US Marine Corps, US Air Force and US Army still carry on a tradition, as did the Royal Navy (until 1970), during formal dining ceremonies where, if anyone is observed to be breaching prescribed etiquette, they receive a 'punishment' whereby they are 'sent to the grog' and publicly made to drink from a toilet bowl containing a concoction of alcoholic drinks designed to have a very unpalatable taste. Teetotallers do not escape – something equally unappealing is mixed for them.

Subsequently, after the decision was made, in January 1970, to discontinue the practice of including rum in naval rations, 11 a.m. on 31 July 1970 would be the last time that the 'Up Spirits' and 'Muster for Rum' would take place on a British naval ship – this date is known as 'The Black Tot Day'. British naval personnel were compensated with an additional can of beer in their rations.

As for the Commonwealth, Australia had stopped serving rum in 1921. However, the Royal Canadian Navy did not stop the practice until 31 March 1972, and the New Zealand Navy held out until 27 February 1990.

The caskets of navy rum that remained after 'Black Tot Day' were put up for auction and were bought up by Chief Petty Officer Brian Cornford, who had served with the Royal Navy submarines during the Second World War. He had the navy drop off their cargo in Gibraltar, where he and John Kania, a cellar master, emptied the barrels into 1-gallon earthenware flagons (1.2 US gallons), wrapped in wicker and date-stamped. The rum was then sold on, mostly to Royal Navy, RAF and British Army messes (plus a few local pubs), and the flagons that remain are now highly sought after (fetching up to £1,250 at auction). Nine years later, entrepreneur Charles Tobias founded Pusser's Rum Ltd (Pusser being Royal Navy slang for a purser, a ship's store master responsible for administering 'the tot') and acquired the rights to produce rum from the original Royal Navy recipe using a blend of five West Indian rums (see Rums of Distinction below).

PUSSER'S GUNPOWDER
STRENGTH 54.5% ABV

In 1979 British Virgin Islands-based entrepreneur Charles Tobias approached the Royal Navy for the rights to produce (or, strictly speaking, reproduce) the British Navy rum ration as a commercial drink under a brand named Pusser's. Tobias obtained the blending information and recipes along with the rights to use the Royal Navy flag on labels and marketing. As part of the deal, Tobias pledged to donate a portion of the profits from every bottle of Pusser's rum sold to the Royal Navy Sailors' Fund. Tobias has kept his word and, alongside donating cases of rum every year to assist with fundraising initiatives, Pusser's is believed to have raised over a quarter of a million pounds for navy charities supporting active and ex-service men and women of the navy. In addition, Pusser's also supports numerous charities worldwide, including the Star & Garter Home in London, the Royal Naval Museum at Portsmouth, the United States Navy Memorial Foundation, the National Maritime Museum in Greenwich, Habitat for Humanity and Island Dolphin Care, among others. Pusser's is also proud to offer an extensive discount for ex-military and present military personnel through the maritime gift and clothing company Nauticalia.

Pusser's rums are a blend of rums sourced from various parts of the Caribbean, although the blending and bottling operation takes place in the British Virgin Islands. The exact source of the rums used in the Pusser's blend is, naturally, a closely guarded secret, with the only description being that it comprises 'predominately wooden pot-stilled distillations'. Various rum connoisseurs have attempted to unravel the code that comprises Pusser's blend and have suggested that the majority of the composition is from aged stocks from distilleries in Guyana and Trinidad (possibly from the Angostura distillery).

When the brand launched in 1980, they produced a 'blue label' navy rum which weighed in at a hefty 54.5 per cent ABV. In 2012, the company launched Original Admiralty Rum at 40 per cent ABV simultaneously with a Gunpowder Strength Rum at 54.5 per cent. This was actually just a cute piece of marketing as the supposedly 'new' Gunpowder Strength Rum was merely the old 'blue label' rebranded. The new 'blue label' Admiralty variety was created so that the brand could supply their product to British naval bases where for health-and-safety reasons spirits above 40 per cent ABV are banned. As is to be expected from a mid-level overproof, Gunpowder Strength benefits from a little water, which brings to the fore the syrupy flavours of the demerara molasses and citrus undertones. Gunpowder Strength is also great with a fiery ginger beer mixer and a dash of lime or in the Painkiller cocktail for which Pusser's owns a trademark registered to their home on the British Virgin Islands (see Appendix: Rum Cocktails).

PART 6

TYPES OF RUM

TOWARDS A GENERAL CLASSIFICATION IN RUM PRODUCTION

Unlike whisky and brandy (and other spirits), there is no single, internationally recognised system for classification for types of rum. One of the principal reasons for this is the sheer variety of different rum styles being produced across the world. Although in popular consciousness rum is synonymous with the Caribbean, in the twenty-first century rum is produced in over fifty countries across the world, all with different regulations and production criteria. The resulting confusion presents the rum enthusiast with a problem: how to differentiate rum styles and flavours from bottle labels.

One traditional approach was to classify rums according to their colour (light rums, dark rums, gold rums etc.) and, whilst this provides a general framework, it is not without its deceptions. There is a misconception that dark rums and darker gold rums get their colour through ageing processes. In fact, many dark rums are unaged, and many light rums are aged and then filtered through charcoal to gain clarity, but let us start with the basics.

As stated numerous times before, rum is produced from the by-products of sugar refining, either cane juice, molasses or cane syrup. In simple terms one of these sugar solutions is mixed with yeast and water to create a 'wash', left to ferment, then distilled, filtered, aged in oak or other wooden barrels for different periods of time and then blended. In each part of the process, however, different rum makers adopt different methods. At the fermentation stage, for example, the time the wash is left to ferment has an impact on the flavour and style of the rum being produced. Light rums undergo a rapid fermentation process of between twenty-four and forty-eight hours prior to distilling, whereas darker heavier rums generally require longer fermentation periods. Once the required fermentation period has been achieved, the wash is then transferred to the still for the distilling stage.

Pot Stills versus Column Stills

Rum is traditionally distilled via two different methods, pot stills and column stills, and this provides a useful descriptor in our search for a general classification for rum. Pot stills are the oldest method, originating from the early rum producers in the seventeenth century, and are still widely used by many rum houses. A pot still is basically a large copper kettle in which the wash is placed and heated. As alcohol has a lower boiling point than water, the vapours produced rise up to the top of the still and into a condenser where they are cooled and converted back into liquid form. Most pot stills are made of copper as the metal conducts heat more efficiently, although some small artisan producers use a mixture of

wooden and copper pots. The first distillation of the wash produces a spirit containing between 25 and 30 per cent ABV. The reason the alcohol level is fairly modest is due to water vapour from the wash rising up to the neck of the still and forming condensation. The solution is then distilled a second time to remove any errant impurities and produce a spirit of 65 per cent plus ABV.

Pot distilling, although the oldest method, is not the most efficient and requires considerable skill and expertise of the distillers to produce the desired style of rum. However, pot distilling gives the distiller licence to experiment with timings and different 'cuts' (the process of removing impurities) and pot-distilled rums in general have a deeper, darker and stronger depth of flavour. One disadvantage of pot distilling is that it is more time-consuming and labour intensive and requires the rum to be produced in batches, which can cause issues with quality control and standardisation of different rums.

The second method of producing rum is by distilling through column stills. The column still was patented by Irish tax inspector turned inventor Aeneas Coffey (1780–1839) and is often referred to as the 'Coffey Still'. The column still's basic design was not actually invented by Coffey himself. It had been patented by a Cork-based whiskey distillery in 1822 but hadn't proved to be very successful. Coffey modified the original design by adding additional columns and other innovations, and he patented his design in 1830. Early Coffey stills produced spirits of about 60 per cent (or somewhat higher) ABV concentration but provided distillers with notable advantages: its fuel costs were low, its output high

(2,000 gallons a day of pure alcohol was a good average), it needed less maintenance and cleaning than pot stills and, because the still was steam-heated, there was no risk whatsoever of scorching (as could occur with pot stills), saving labour costs and distillation downtime. Modern versions of the Coffey still can achieve much higher alcohol concentrations, approaching 95.6 per cent alcohol. As alcohol forms an azeotrope (constant boiling point) with water at this level of concentration, it is impossible to achieve higher purity alcohol by distillation alone.

The different advantages of column stills over pot stills and vice versa are a matter of individual preference and considerable debate. There is no doubt that the introduction of the Coffey still in the nineteenth century industrialised rum production on a scale that had not been possible previously. Multiple column stills provide greater control over the distillate produced and generally produce lighter rums with a cleaner taste. Column-still rum production in geographical terms occurs most prominently on Spanish-speaking islands in the Caribbean such as Cuba, the Dominican Republic and Puerto Rico, and also in Panama. Traditional pot-distilled rums tend to be produced on English-speaking islands, most notably Jamaica where the nuances of the pot-distilling processes are granted the prestige of one of the 'dark arts'. Barbados rum distillers are a mix of both pot- and column-still operations and often combine both processes in their blended rums.

Maturation in Oak

The ageing of rum is a complex process and traditionally takes place in wooden (usually oak) barrels. Ever since
rum has been produced it has been stored and transported
in barrels, moving from trading point to trading point, on
merchant ships and naval vessels, from sugar plantation to
distillery and so on. The ease of transportation and storage
was one of the initial considerations for using oak barrels for
rum, but as rum producers became more sophisticated, rum
ageing has developed into a science in itself.

The choice of oak is key in the maturation process as the
wood, in a sense, is left to breathe. This means that air and
vapour can move freely inside and outside the barrel whilst
retaining the liquid safely in a watertight container. Most
of the barrels used in the production of spirits are made in
the United States (where they are used to make bourbon) or
France and Spain (where they are used to age sherry, wine
and brandies). Many rum producers import second-hand
barrels made of white oak from the United States. The regulations around the production of bourbon in America forbid
the refilling of oak barrels once they have been emptied for
bottling and so Caribbean rum producers have access to a
supply of cheap second-hand oak barrels on their doorstep.
American white oak trees (*Quercus alba*) grow much faster
than European red oak (*Quercus robur*), making them more
notably sustainable. Bourbon barrels are charred before
being filled (the inside of the barrel is scorched with flames
to remove potentially harmful wood resins and to produce
a lining of charcoal-like carbon. European barrels used to

age cognac or sherry achieve the same result through a gentler toasting process. Unsurprisingly, the type of oak barrel used to age rum and its origin and residual flavour from the ageing of previous spirits adds noticeably different flavours to the rums. Bourbon white oak barrels promote vanilla and chocolate flavours to a rum whereas the European sherry and brandy casks add spiciness and tannins.

The type of barrel used is not the only variable in the ageing of rum, however. The age of the barrel can have a profound effect on the flavour and colour of a rum. Newer barrels impart flavours quicker than older barrels that have been refilled several times. For this reason, a three-year-old rum aged in a fresh white oak barrel will taste markedly different from the same rum aged for the same amount of time in an older barrel. The choice of barrel is therefore of paramount importance in the ageing process as, for example, a hefty pot-still-produced dark rum needs longer to mature, whereas lighter, column-still rums can deteriorate and develop an overly oaky flavour if left for too long.

The climate in which rums are matured also has a considerable effect on the flavours and colours imparted through the ageing process. As the cask breathes over time, particularly in hot climates, the liquid inside starts to evaporate. In particularly hot countries in central and southern America, up to 50 per cent of a five-year-aged rum will have been lost to evaporation. Evaporation is also an issue in Caribbean islands although this can also vary from island to island, as even subtle shifts in climate such as humidity and air pressure can make notable differences to the ageing process. High levels of humidity can also accelerate maturation, so in effect a three-year-aged rum matured on Barbados would taste remarkably different from a rum matured in a more temperate climate in Europe. The discrepancies in measuring ageing times therefore is something to consider when choosing aged rums, and careful consideration should be given to the climate where the rum was produced.

The Fine Art of Blending

Almost all rums are blended, the process by which different ages of rum casks are combined and mixed to create styles and flavours. This can include blends of pot-distilled and column-distilled casks and casks produced by different distilleries. It is a matter of searching for balance and an overall consistency of volume and style.

The process is akin to selecting complementary grape varieties that are used to create a blended wine. The blender hand-selects the rum barrels that will be used in a particular blend based on their varying ages, types and styles of rum, each adding a distinctive layer of character to the final blend. The master blender has an expert's sense of smell and palate. In most countries, in order to be classified as rum, the distillate must be aged for at least a year (two years minimum in Cuba). The selection process and careful balancing of the blend is a fine art. Young column-still casks impart a fresh, clean flavour whereas older pot-still casks add depth and colour. By way of example, Havana Club adhere to a system in regard to their blending policy. Their column-still single distillate is aged for two years and then blended with a high-strength *aguardiente* produced from molasses. By varying the ratio between the two elements they have the base for their rums and have the flexibility to combine and recombine with other aged casks to produce rums of different depth, volume and style.

Classifications of Rum

As mentioned before, there is no international classification of rum as there is with brandy and whisky. However, it is possible to differentiate between rum styles using different criteria. These include the base material the rum has been produced from, i.e. molasses, cane syrup or cane juice. Has the rum been aged and, if so, for how long? How has the rum been distilled – by pot still or column still? How many, if any, separate rums have contributed to the blend?

These questions then branch out into further distinctions, which can be separated by the following descriptors:

Single pot-still rum: a rum that is pot distilled and is the product of only one distillery.
Single column-still rum: a rum produced by column still and is the product of only one distillery.
Single blended rum: a mixture of both pot-distilled and column-distilled rums from a single distillery.
Blended rum: a pot-distilled blend that uses casks produced by more than one distillery.
Multi-column rum: a rum blended from column-distilled casks from more than one distillery.

Each of the above descriptors can then be applied to the following 'styles' of rum:

Light/white rums: Usually column distilled and characterised by a lightness of flavour, often filtered after maturation to achieve clarity.

Dark rums: Pot distilled from molasses with a stronger depth of flavour and subjected to a more complex maturation and blending process.

Rhum Agricole: Distinctive to French-speaking parts of the Caribbean and produced on Haiti, Martinique and Guadeloupe. Rhum Agricole is produced from cane juice and column distilled.

Gold/amber rums: The halfway point between light and dark rums, medium-bodied and aged blends that can be a mix of both pot-distilled and column-distilled rums.

Overproof/navy rums: Not for the faint-hearted and containing a much higher ABV than the standard 40 per cent of most rums. There are two standards for overproof: navy proof rum is typically bottled at 57 per cent alcohol, or 114 proof, and 151 rum, which is bottled at 75.5 per cent alcohol, or 151 proof. Overproof can be produced either by column stills, which have the capacity to yield higher alcohol content more efficiently, or by pot stills, which is more time-consuming but still possible.

Premium rums: Usually aged for many years, a masterfully blended concoction of different casks and styles to produce high-quality rum with distinctive character and complex balance of flavours. Can be either pot distilled or column distilled, or a blend of both.

Spiced/flavoured rums: The principal flavours are added after blending and tend to be sweet due to addition of sugar and caramel and fruit flavourings. Some take amber rums as their base, but many use cheap white rum that is then artificially coloured. Many rum enthusiasts argue that commercially produced, flavoured or spiced rums aren't actually rums at all but hybrid liqueurs.

The rums presented below and judiciously placed throughout this book where they relate to a particular moment in rum's timeline can be referenced against the categorisation system above.

ST NICHOLAS ABBEY 18-YEAR-OLD

RUMS
OF
DISTINCTION

St Nicholas Abbey Distillery on Barbados has something of an oxymoronic distinction to its name in being both the youngest and (possibly) the oldest distillery on the island. The modern brand and rum-making operation dates from 2009, when the current owners, the Warren family, first started bottling a brand of premium rum before developing their own distillery in 2013. The estate itself, however, complete with its imposing Jacobean mansion house, dates from the mid-seventeenth century, as does its recently revived sugar plantation. The story of the estate is one of intrigue, love and dark dealings, and it is a pivotal part of Barbadian history.

Business 'partners' Lieutenant-Colonel Benjamin Berringer (?–1660) and Sir John Yeamans (1611–1674) owned two adjacent sugar plantations on Barbados: the Berringer Plantation to the north, and Yeaman's Plantation, known as Greenland, to the south. Although allegedly 'partners', tensions between the two men came to a head over the actual size of, and the boundaries between, the two plantations, which in total came to nearly 400 acres of land. Berringer hailed from an influential aristocratic family in England and arrived in Barbados in 1624. His success as a planter had made him wealthy and he dabbled in politics as a member of the Barbados Council, making him a figure of considerable influence in the developing colony. Berringer also built the famous Jacobean mansion house for his family in 1658, which remains one of only three surviving Jacobean-style mansions in the Caribbean region (it is now a museum and tourist attraction).

John Yeamans came to Barbados later than Berringer, around 1650. An ex-army officer without his 'partner's' aristocratic connections, he was something of a chancer and ruthless in his business dealings. At some point the two men fell out, possibly over Yeamans' land-grabbing but most likely over a very public courting by Yeamans of Berringer's beautiful young wife Margaret.

Benjamin Berringer died in mysterious circumstances in 1660. One account tells of him leaving Margaret after confronting her about her relationship with Yeamans and travelling to Speightstown to file to have their marriage annulled. Whilst in Speightstown, Berringer was poisoned by an assassin hired by Yeamans and died at the house of a family friend. A conflicting, and more romantic, account has Berringer shot by Yeamans in a duel. Either way, the Berringer family smelt a rat, particularly when Margaret married Yeamans three months after her husband's death. Having acquired Berringer's estate through the marriage, Yeamans amalgamated the two plantations and named it, with remarkable hubris, Yeamans' Plantation.

Yeamans continued to prosper both financially and politically despite the scandal (Berringer's murder was investigated but no charges were brought against Yeamans) and was rewarded for his Royalist leaning after the Restoration with a baronetcy. In 1663 Yeamans sailed to America and founded a fledgling colony in South Carolina, appointing himself governor in the process. Yeamans returned to Barbados in 1669 due to failing health and died on his plantation in 1674. On the death of his wife Margaret a few years later, ownership of the estate fell to Berringer's daughter, who reputedly despised Yeamans, and changed the name to the Nicholas Plantation, presumably after her husband George Nicholas.

The Nicholas family continued to run the plantation until a crash in sugar prices in the 1720s forced them to sell the estate to Joseph Dottin (1690–1735), the deputy governor of Barbados. Dottin already owned several estates on Barbados and had set a precedent by gifting them to his daughters on occasion of their marriage. Although Joseph Dottin died in 1735, his wishes were realised when his youngest daughter Christian married Sir John Gay Alleyne, thereby inheriting the Nicholas estate.

Sir John Alleyne was a significant figure in Barbados history (see Rums of Distinction: Mount Gay 1703 Black Barrel) and set about modernising the plantation. Sir John is credited with expanding the estate's rum distillery and production of sugar and molasses, and with developing lucrative export ties with Europe and America. At its height, the Nicholas Plantation was one of the most successful in the Caribbean.

Christian Dottin died 1782 and Sir John married his cousin Abel Alleyne, and promptly fathered several children who he assumed would inherit the estate. However, on Sir John's death in 1801, it was discovered that his first wife's will had stipulated that the estate should be passed to members of the Dottin family. Unfortunately, Christian and Sir John's only child had died aged 12 in a bizarre accident whilst at school at Eton. The estate remained in probate while a search was made for members of the Dottin family who may have legitimate claims and fell into debt and disrepair, eventually being repossessed by the Chancery Court in 1810.

The estate was purchased for £20,500, the sum of the amassed debts, by real estate prospectors Edward and Lawrence Cumberbatch. Edward's son Edward Jr stood to inherit the plantation on his father's death. However, again legal technicalities interfered and threw a spanner in the works: Edward Sr had stipulated in his will that his son would only acquire the family real-estate assets if he refrained from marrying his 'true love', Mary Ashe, the daughter of a travelling minstrel from Bath, for a minimum of five years following his father's death. Edward Sr clearly believed that the lure of considerable wealth and assets would cause his son's ardour to wane during the five-year hiatus of their affair. Edward was, by all accounts, something of a black sheep of the family, whose recklessness cavorting with unsuitable people dismayed his family. However, the gentleman was not for turning and defied his family's wishes and married his sweetheart Mary, thereby forfeiting any claim on the estate – a romantic tale that could grace the pages of a novel by Thomas Hardy or Winston Graham.

Eventually the estate passed to Edward Sr's daughter Sarah Cumberbatch and her husband Charles Cave. It is thought that Sarah and Charles gave the estate its current name by combining the name of the Cumberbatch ancestral home, 'St Nicholas Parish', with 'Bath Abbey', where the couple were married. The Cave family had considerable banking interests and had the business acumen to run the estate profitably for over 100 years. The implementation of steam-powered mills in 1890 made St Nicholas Abbey rise again as one of the key sugar producers on Barbados. However, increased global competition in the sugar trade resulted in falling profits and the refinery closed in 1947, with the estate and historic Jacobean mansion turned into a tourist attraction.

In 2006, St Nicholas Abbey estate was purchased by Larry Warren, a well-known local architect who made it his personal project to restore not only the mansion but also the plantation to its former glory. The Warren family have overseen a meticulous restoration of the mansion house, which is now a museum and visitor centre, replanted sugar cane, refurbished the steam mill and rebuilt the distillery.

Larry's son Simon oversees the distillery side of the project and initially enlisted the help of master blender Richard Searle from the nearby Foursquare Distillery. Among the first rums released by St Nicholas Abbey was the premium St Nicholas Abbey 18-Year-Old. Understandably, it takes time to bed in a thriving sugar plantation and even longer to build up stocks of maturing casks for blending, and so, in order to get St Nicholas Abbey distillery up and running, Richard Searle 'loaned' casks from Foursquare's prodigious cellars and oversaw the creation of the first rums.

Since then, however, St Nicholas' plantation has flourished, and the estate is now producing and bottling two rums made on site from entirely their own produce and materials: a clear Bajan-style white rum and a five-year-aged variety blended from their own maturing stocks. As a business, the distillery is a model of sustainability and self-sufficiency with virtually every aspect of production undertaken by hand and in house. Cane from the plantation is cut by hand and milled in the restored steam-driven sugar mill, which is in turn powered by home-made bagasse bio-fuel briquettes left over from extracting the cane juice. The boiler that heats the steam-heated pot still/column still hybrid (named 'Annabelle' for no apparent reason) and evaporators is also fuelled by bagasse. St Nicholas Abbey's rums are distilled from cane syrup (although they are experimenting with molasses too), produced by boiling down the cane juice to approximately 70 per cent ABV, which preserves stocks for year-round production. Even the bottling takes place on site, with hand-stencilled labels and leather seals and stamps lovingly applied by St Nicholas Abbey's dedicated staff. The only aspect of production not done in house is the importing of traditional ex-bourbon ageing barrels from the US. However, it would be no surprise to see in the future the Warren family planting sustainable oak tree stocks and setting up a coopering and toasting element to their operations.

All this points to a very bright future for Barbados' youngest distillery ... Oh, but wait a minute, any readers who have been paying attention will no doubt want to know what the oxymoron relating to St Nicholas Abbey's Distillery is? Shortly after purchasing the estate in 2006, the Warren family entered into a partnership with US University, the College of William and Mary, to undertake extensive archaeological research around the St Nicholas Abbey estate. Initially, the work was to gather information to help with accurate restoration work, but the programme has expanded and now provides artefacts for the estate museum and education centre. The current aims of the project are to gather enough information to assist with painting a fuller picture of the lives of plantation workers, be they slaves or slave owners, and create a permanent educational exhibition. During the course of various 'digs' around the estate, thousands of artefacts have been unearthed, including fragments of enamel-lined tin and copper pots and earthenware that could prove rum, or something close to rum, was being produced at St Nicholas Abbey as early as the 1650s, thereby making it a rival to Mount Gay's title of oldest surviving rum distillery in the Caribbean.

St Nicholas Abbey's rums are only available from the plantation gift shop or online via a handful of selected suppliers. As they are relatively small-batch rums produced by painstakingly traditional methods, they are expensive, with the cheapest Over Proof White retailing at around £60 a bottle. The real jewel, however, is the highly collectable 18-Year-Old premium, which is in short supply – stocks will start to disappear over the next few years. The reason for this is that, as mentioned above, it is produced from Foursquare Distillery's casks and eventually St Nicholas Abbey will be producing extra-aged rums from their own developing stocks. For this reason, the retail prices start at around £200 a bottle and will no doubt rise as the stocks of the original Richard Searle blend become increasingly rare. An amber rum, with hints of tobacco and watermelon, the 18-Year-Old has just the right balance between sharpness and sweetness with a fruity, citrus finish. If you have £200 to spend on a bottle of rum, this could prove to be a very shrewd investment as it will undoubtedly be a very sought-after collector's item in the future.

APPLETON ESTATE 12-YEAR-OLD RARE BLEND/WRAY AND NEPHEW WHITE OVERPROOF

Appleton Estate towers above all challengers in terms of Jamaican rum. The estate itself is located in the south-western region of the island, in an area renowned for its unique scenery and geology. All of the rum produced by Appleton is from the different varieties of sugar cane grown on their 1,000-acre plantation. The local environment is a key element in Appleton folklore as the estate is surrounded by the karst rock formations of Cockpit County and flanked by Jamaica's only surviving rainforest. Karst is a topography formed from the dissolution of soluble rocks such as limestone, dolomite and gypsum. It is characterised by underground drainage systems with sinkholes and caves, which provide a unique water basin perfect for irrigating the mineral-rich soil the cane is grown in. Furthermore, the surrounding forests help to create a unique microclimate, and during the wet season when sugar cane is thriving it is said in Cockpit County you can almost set your watch by the time of day the heavens open to water the thirsty crops. In short, the unique environment in which Appleton's rums are produced is as close to a *terroir* as any rum can lay legitimate claim.

The earliest known deeds to the estate date back to the mid- eighteenth century and cite a modest plantation of some

10 acres. The estate was owned by a former British naval officer Frances Dickinson who was part of William Penn's invasion force of 1655. The estate passed through various hands until it was bought by J. Wray and Nephew in 1916, in whose hands it notionally still belongs.

The J. Wray and Nephew company dates back to the early nineteenth century when original owner John Wray bought a pub in Kingstown and started to blend his own rums. By the end of the century, the company (now run by John Wray's eponymous nephew) was producing award-winning rums of considerable repute. With an eye for clever marketing, Wray and Nephew were amongst the first to experiment with extra-aged premium rum marques, quickly establishing a formidable reputation. Amongst their most successful rums was Wray and Nephew 17 (year aged), which provided the base for the famous Mai Tai cocktail. Although this line was discontinued many years ago, a few vintage bottles are still in circulation but sell at auction for around £20,000 each.

J. Wray and Nephew were taken over by the Campari Group drinks multinational in 2012 and, besides the distillery on the Appleton Estate in Cockpit County, they run a sister operation at the New Yarmouth plantation – a sugar refinery that dates from the early eighteenth century and was at one time owned by the Earl of Dudley and British Foreign Secretary John William Ward (1781–1833). Situated in central south Jamaica, the New Yarmouth distillery is devoted largely to producing Wray and Nephew white rums (with a selection of lesser-known brands) and their signature Wray and Nephew White Overproof. As far as overproofs go – and this is not for the faint of heart at 63 per cent ABV – Wray and Nephew is commendably dry with fruity tones.

It is best taken either with a little watering and a slice of lime, with Jamaican ginger beer or in a weapons-grade Daiquiri.

Appleton Estate 12-Year-Old Rare Blend is a marvel, although in truth all Appleton Estate rums are of exceptional quality. After a thirty-six-hour fermentation using their own proprietary yeast and limestone-filtered mineral water, the rum is pot distilled and sent to Wray and Nephew's cavernous warehouse of ageing casks in Kingston where it sits ageing for a minimum of twelve years before being blended by the legendary Joy Spence, the first female master blender in the world. Oaky chocolate notes prevail with hints of vanilla and coffee, all undercut by Appleton's signature orange-peel bouquet – a product, according to Joy Spence, of the unique eco-environment of the Appleton Estate. It is quite simply the best mid-range extra-aged rum on the market and rightfully regarded in Jamaica as a national treasure.

GOSLING'S BLACK SEAL

Bermuda's iconic rum brand Gosling's Black Seal is not the product of a distillery on the island but the product of 150 years of expertise at the hands of master blenders.

In 1806, London-based liquor trader James Gosling gathered together his savings, sold his business and decided to 'light out' for the territories of the New World. Gosling's initial plan was to emigrate to Virginia, America, and set up business; to this end he chartered a ship, *Mercury*, loaded with £10,000 of wines and spirits, and set sail. Unfortunately, the journey wasn't a happy one: *Mercury* was initially hit by ferocious Atlantic storms and left drifting on becalmed seas for several weeks whilst on-board repairs were made and the boat patched up. Gosling had only taken out a ninety-day charter for the ship and by the ninety-sixth day of floating around the Atlantic, the charter company lost patience and headed to the nearest port, which happened to be Hamilton, Bermuda, and set Gosling and his stocks (or what remained of them) ashore.

James Gosling and his brother Ambrose, who accompanied him, must have liked what they saw on Bermuda as they shelved plans to go to America, opting instead to set up their business on the island instead. In December 1806 they registered their company Gosling Brothers Ltd and opened a store on Front Street, Hamilton, which became a Bermudian icon and the company headquarters for 130 years.

At first, the Gosling brothers were merely liquor traders but by the mid 1850s they had started experimenting with blending rums imported from distilleries on other Caribbean islands. In 1860 their Gosling's Old Rum was launched. Up until the First World War the only way to buy Gosling's was either by the barrel or to take an empty bottle to the Gosling's store for a fill up. However, as the popularity of the rum spread and demand increased, the Goslings hit upon a novel way of bottling their products for commercial sale.

The British Navy had established a base on Bermuda in the early 1800s, primarily to protect British interests from intrusions from French privateers. The Goslings supplied liquor and wine to the officers' mess on the base and so struck a buy-back deal for empty heavy-set wine bottles, which they recycled by filling them with rum from their barrels, putting in cork stoppers and sealing with black wax.

The Goslings noticed the tendency of customers entering their shop to point at bottles of Old Rum on the shelves and request 'the bottle with the black seal'. Hence a quick name change was in order, along with the creation of the famous label logo depicting a black seal (the sea mammal) juggling a barrel of rum with the tip of its nose. Bermudans are rightly proud of their rum which holds a hallowed place at the very heart of the island's culture, so much so that when Bermuda hosted the 2017 America's Cup yacht racing series it was given the title 'Official Spirit of the America Cup'. The company also branch out into a range of maritime-related clothing and leisurewear lines, and it is impossible to walk down a street in Hamilton without passing somebody proudly sporting a baseball cap adorned with the Black Seal logo. A local folk tradition on Bermuda, known as 'wetting the roof', takes place whenever the construction of a new building is completed. This is basically an excuse for a good old shindig (they like a party on Bermuda!) but also involves breaking a bottle of, you guessed it, Gosling's Black Seal and pouring it on the roof to bless the premises.

Although regularly lauded at International Spirits competitions and winning multiple medals, up until recently the only way of buying Gosling's was to visit Bermuda. I have been lucky enough to have been aware of Gosling's through a close family friend, Joseph Christopher (see Introduction), and it has long been puzzling me why the company haven't got their export business together. This is all due to change in the near future, with Gosling's striking deals with importers in North America and other parts of the Caribbean, and plans afoot to expand into Europe.

Gosling's currently produces three main varieties of rum, alongside various limited editions: the traditional iconic Black Seal dark rum, a recently launched Gosling's Gold Amber rum and the modern incarnation of Old Rum (presented in a champagne bottle with a black wax seal).

Black Seal is a blend of three different distillates aged independently from distilleries on Jamaica, in Guyana and Barbados. The casks are shipped to Bermuda and blended and bottled on the island so, although the claim to Bermuda rum that adorns the label isn't strictly true, the blend is a closely guarded family recipe dating back 150 years and, anyhow, it's so great it is churlish to split hairs about these matters: the blend is the key.

The blend for both the Black Seal and Old Rum varieties, with the latter benefiting from extra ageing in white oak barrels, is a mix of predominately column-still rum from Guyana and

Barbados with a wily dash of pot-still rum from Jamaica that gives Gosling's rums their startling balance and depth. The Black Seal remains the best-seller, and rightfully so. If something isn't broke, don't fix it, and the deep treacly tones are perfectly suited to a Dark 'n' Stormy (mixed with ginger beer) or sipped with ice and twist of fresh lime.

DIPLOMATICO RESERVA EXTRA ANEJO

At the time of writing Venezuela is teetering on the brink of civil war. This makes me very sad. I have only had the privilege to visit Venezuela on one occasion yet retain very fond memories of my time there, particularly the warmth, dry humour and kindness of the people I met and befriended. It is hard, even if you haven't had the pleasure of visiting this fantastic country, not to feel empathy for Venezuela. A country that has been terminally bullied by imperial/colonial greed throughout modern history yet sits on some of the most potentially lucrative mineral resources in South America nevertheless still has nothing to show for it. Meanwhile, the hawks and buzzards of global capitalism – faceless multinational corporations, hedge-fund managers and the *oily* industries – circle hungrily above. It is scant consolation under the (current) circumstances, and I'm really not being glib, but Venezuela does have something to be very proud about and that is their excellent rum.

Destilerias Unides S.A., or DUSA for short, was established in 1959 as a merger of several, largely struggling at the time, small Venezuelan distilleries. The main mover and shaker behind the merger was Seagram's (see The Bootleggers Behind Captain Morgan Rum) who retained a controlling share.

The DUSA distillery in the town of La Miel on the north-east plains of the Andes is enormous, covering over 30 acres of land.

When Seagram went belly-up, Diageo pounced but didn't gain control of the distillery. Instead they struck a deal whereby they could market the Cacique brand (the only reason Seagram's were interested in the first place) worldwide as long as the distillery remained, to all intents and purposes, 100 per cent under Venezuelan ownership.

Whilst Cacique produce fine rums – they are amongst the best-selling brands in South America – it is the Diplomatico brand that really floats the boat, particularly for drinkers with a sweet tooth. A careful blend of both pot-distilled (unusually for a South American distillery, DUSA has several pot stills) but mostly column-distilled rum from extra-aged casks, Diplomatico Reserva Extra Anejo is a marvel. Some critics have said, rather dismissively, that it is too sweet (additional sugar syrup is added during ageing), but I don't agree. It is very strong on vanilla tones (again the naysayers suggest it's only good for pouring on ice cream) and by personal preference I wouldn't use it in a cocktail. However, if sipped over ice and left to breathe from the bottle, it is extraordinary. Think of all the things you loved when you were a kid – candy floss, chocolate, vanilla ice cream – and then throw in adult tastes like strong coffee and chilli, and you get somewhere near to assessing this fantastic rum. As I referenced as *diplomatico-ally* as I could at the start of this appraisal, Venezuela is in trouble and supporting this fine, home-produced product – and to my taste one of the finest rums in South America – may go some small way to speed them on the road to recovery.

OLD MONK 7 YEAR 42.8%

India is a huge market for rum and spirits. I attended the wedding of a Sikh friend, which with its fascinating parade of rituals and ceremonies was a thrilling experience. The after party was awash with spirits and it was here that I discovered Old Monk 7 Year. At one point the top-selling brand in the world – but then again in a country of 1.5 billion people this shouldn't be a surprise – Old Monk has only recently been surpassed by McDowell's No. 1, another Indian brand and far inferior. Old Monk has heritage that McDowell's slightly erroneously can claim, but never mind; Old Monk is a finer rum and wins hands down.

In 1855, an entrepreneurial Scotsman named Edward Abraham Dyer, father of Colonel Reginald Edward Harry Dyer of Jallianwala Bagh massacre, set up a brewery in Kasauli, Himachal Pradesh, to cater to the British requirement for cheap beer. This brewery changed hands and became a distillery by the name of Mohan Meakin Pvt. Ltd.

Old Monk, purportedly a creation of Ved Rattan Mohan, a keen rum enthusiast and blender of fine spirits and the managing director of Mohan Meakin Ltd, was first introduced in India in the 1960s. Before Old Monk, there was Hercules rum (which still exists) that was distilled exclusively for the Indian armed forces. Superior in taste and perhaps even in quality to Hercules (as loyalists believe), the brand soon became one of the leading dark rums in the world and the most popular IMFL (Indian-Made

Foreign Liquor) brand in the country. The affordable pricing strategy has also worked in their favour. There was a time when Old Monk dominated the rum market. There were other brands but none came close in quality or popularity. About 8 million bottles were sold annually in the early part of the twenty-first century. However, the rise of other brands and the ease with which more 'exotic' or 'authentic' rums have been imported into India have led to a marked decrease in domestic sales of Old Monk. This led to industry rumours that the brand, unless it could find an enthusiastic buyer (Diageo, Bacardi, Campari, Green's – take your pick of multinational drinks corporations), was going to be discontinued. However, Old Monk prevails, at least for the foreseeable future.

Old Monk 7 Year is quite heavy for a dark rum, due to the thick molasses it is refined from in the Ghaziabad Distillery in Uttar Pradesh, the northern Indian state most famous for the Taj Mahal. It is a bittersweet rum, not without its merits at all, but an acquired taste. If you like dark chocolate and the smell of cloves you'll love it.

I personally have a lot of respect for Old Monk but confess there are other similar rums I'd rather drink by preference. Nonetheless, it is a rum of distinction and I would certainly never steer anyone away from it (as I might with some awful commercial 'spiced' rums such as Sailor Jerry, named after a former US Navy officer turned tattoo 'artist' from Nevada named Norman who ended his seafaring days living on Hawaii – please explain to me what is going on there).

TRES HOMBRES 8-YEAR-AGED RHUM AGRICOLE

My wife, Joanna Taylor, put me on to this rum and it is a bit left field, to say the least, but may be the future and seems a pertinent point to leave this whistle-stop tour of the history of rum – going back to basics, so to speak.

In 2007 three Dutch sailors, Arjen van der Veen, Jorne Langelaan and Andreas Lackner, started converting an old Second World War German minesweeper into a three-mast sailing cargo ship. The *Tres Hombres* vision was to start Europe's first emission-free shipping company.

In 2010, the three Dutch *buccaneers* released their first, and totally unique, rum: an aged *rhum agricole* from the Dominican Republic under the Tres Hombres name. Why is it unique? Well, for a start they enlisted the help of a master blender from Cuba, who remains anonymous, but surely must have some connection to Havana Club or is moonlighting from another distillery. Secondly, they only release as much as they can carry on their boat on one gruelling four-month journey, old-school style, from the Caribbean back to the Netherlands. Thirdly, each year the rum they produce is different from the previous year, creating a series of limited-edition vintages that can never and will never be repeated. Their rums sell out very quickly and they have established a cult following based on the unique selling point that it is transported in the way rum was always traditionally shipped around the world. The winds and vagaries of climate and the anarchy of the oceans all add to the process and ultimately the end product.

The *Tres Hombres* – Arjen van der Veen, Jorne Langelaan and Andreas Lackner, also take on interns, who can travel with them on their journey to and from various islands as they source their annual 'edition', and one expects meet who the mysterious master blender is. If I was a younger man, and fitter than I am (they make you work for your board and the experience, which is fair enough) and could swim better and didn't have 'responsibilities', I'd jump at the chance to board their beautiful three-sail schooner and act out every pirate fantasy from my childhood imagination. Imagine sailing across the Atlantic like Christopher Columbus ... I can but go to bed and dream of such an opportunity when my head hits the pillow at night. Although, in truth, I'm not that great on boats and get 'cabin fever' on cross-Channel ferries when I can't see dry land.

The bottle my wife found for me is their 2016 8-Year-Aged Rhum Agricole, a column-distilled blend from the Dominican Republic distilled, as all *rhum agricoles* are, from cane sugar. It weighs in at a lumpy 44 per cent ABV and that extra alcohol content adds to its citrus sharpness, although it has a heartening warmth in the afterglow. I haven't tried to mix it with anything and, to be honest, wish I'd never broken the lovely handmade rope and wax in the first place as it's a collector's item.

All in all, though, the *Tres Hombres* can only be admired for their fortitude and free thinking and applauded for their tenacity and intelligence in starting Europe's only emission-free shipping company in the modern world. It seems only right that rum is the first product they are moving across the world. Moving back in time to go forward once more.

APPENDIX

RUM COCKTAILS

AROUND THE WORLD

1 dash rum
1 dash vodka
1 dash gin
1 dash tequila
1 dash triple sec
1 dash peach schnapps
1 dash Midori
1 dash blue Curaçao
1 dash 151 rum
1 dash amaretto
1 dash Malibu
1 dash Southern Comfort
1 dash Chambord
1 dash sour mix
1 dash orange juice
1 dash pineapple juice
1 dash cranberry juice
1 dash lemon-lime soda

Fill glass with cracked ice.
Add alcohol and even parts of
sour mix, orange, pineapple
and cranberry juices and
lemon-lime soda.
Blend ingredients.
Serve in tall glass.

BAHAMA MAMA

1.5 oz coconut rum
1.5 oz dark rum
Splash orange juice
Splash pineapple juice
Dash grenadine
Orange wedge
Maraschino cherry

Shake with ice.
Serve into a hurricane glass.
Garnish with an orange wedge
and maraschino cherry.

BOSTON SIDECAR

1.5 oz light rum
0.5 oz brandy
0.5 oz triple sec

Combine all the ingredients in
a shaker filled with ice.
Shake well and strain into a
martini glass.

CARDINAL SIN PUNCH

1 bottle champagne
1 pint dark rum
8 oz sweet vermouth
2 quarts claret
1 quart club soda
6 oz powdered sugar
3 cups lemon juice
6 slices orange
6 slices lemon

Combine all but the
champagne and soda with ice
and stir.
Add ice cubes, club soda and
champagne.
Serves 12.

CARIBBEAN SEA

1.5 oz spiced rum
0.5 oz blue Curaçao
1.5 oz coconut cream
3 oz pineapple juice
Pineapple wedge

Mix in blender with half a cup
of ice. Blend until smooth.
Garnish with pineapple wedge.

CHAMBORLADA

1 oz Chambord
0.5 oz light rum
0.5 oz dark rum
3 oz pineapple juice
2 oz cream of coconut
Pineapple wedge

Combine all ingredients,
except Chambord and
pineapple, with ice in blender.
Blend.
Pour the Chambord into the
bottom of a wine glass.
Pour the blended colada
mixture on top.
Top off with a little more
Chambord.
Garnish with pineapple wedge.

COCO LOCO

0.25 oz dark rum
0.25 oz coconut rum
0.5 oz cream of coconut
0.5 oz papaya juice
0.5 oz orange juice
0.5 oz pineapple juice
0.25 oz grenadine
Pineapple wedge

Blend with ice until smooth.
Garnish with pineapple wedge.

COSMOPOLITANO

1.5 oz white rum
0.5 oz triple sec
0.75 oz cranberry juice
0.25 oz lime juice
Lime peel

Combine all ingredients
in cocktail shaker with ice.
Shake well.
Strain into a cocktail glass.
Garnish with lime peel.

DAY IN THE SHADE

1 oz spice rum
1 oz pineapple juice
0.5 oz cranberry juice

Shake with ice.
Strain into chilled
cocktail glass.

EL PRESIDENTE

2 oz dark rum
4 oz orange juice
Dash grenadine
Maraschino cherry
Orange peel

Shake with ice.
Strain into cocktail glass.
Garnish with maraschino
cherry and orange peel.

HAMMERHEAD

0.5 oz spiced rum
0.5 oz light rum
0.5 oz Malibu
0.5 oz vodka
0.5 oz grenadine
2 oz orange juice
1 oz pineapple juice
Pineapple wedge

Combine all but grenadine and pineapple with ice and stir.
Float grenadine on top.
Garnish with a pineapple wedge.

JAMAICA GLOW

1.5 oz dry gin
1 tbsp Jamaican rum
0.5 oz red wine
2 tbsp orange juice
Lemon wedge

Combine with ice. Shake.
Strain over crushed ice.
Garnish with lemon wedge.

LIMEY

2 oz light rum
1 oz lime liqueur
0.5 oz triple sec
1 tablespoon lime juice
1 cup crushed ice
Lime twist

Blend ingredients except lime twist in a blender filled with 1 cup ice.
Pour into a chilled red wine glass.
Garnish with the lime twist.

LONG ISLAND ICED TEA

0.75 oz rum
0.75 oz gin
0.75 oz vodka
0.75 oz tequila
0.75 oz triple sec
0.75 oz sour mix
Splash cola
Lemon wedge

Shake liquors with sour mix.
Pour into hurricane glass.
Add splash of cola.
Garnish with lemon wedge.

MALIBU

0.75 oz spiced rum
0.25 oz vodka
Orange juice

Build over ice in
highball glass.

MANGO DAIQUIRI

1.5 oz light rum
1 tbsp triple sec
1.5 oz lime juice
1 tbsp sugar
2 oz pureed mango
Half cup crushed ice

Blend with 1 cup crushed ice.
Pour in a cocktail glass.

MOJITO

2 oz white rum
Splash club soda
1/2 tsp icing sugar
Mint leaves

Mix mint leaves with
icing sugar.
Add ice, rum and top with
club soda.
Garnish with a sprig of
fresh mint.

PLANTERS PUNCH

1.5 oz rum
0.75 oz triple sec
Splash dark rum
Splash sour mix
2 oz pineapple juice
2 oz orange juice
Dash grenadine
Orange slice

Shake all except dark rum and
orange slace. Pour over ice in
hurricane glass.
Float dark rum on top.
Garnish with orange slice.

RUM HIGHBALL

2 oz white or dark rum
Ginger ale to fill
Lemon peel

Pour rum into glass over ice.
Fill with ginger ale.
Garnish with lemon peel.

TIDAL WAVE

1 oz 151 rum
1 oz spiced rum
1 oz vodka
Splash sour mix
Splash cranberry juice

Shake with ice.
Strain into shot glass.

ACKNOWLEDGEMENTS

I would like to thank the following people for their invaluable help and support in getting this book off the ground:

Chrissy McMorris (Commissioning Editor), Jezz Palmer and Alexandra Waite (Project Editors,) and Katie Beard (Designer) at The History Press.

Aubrey Smith for his lovely illustrations.

My 'rum advisors' Leonard 'Lenny' Hamilton and William Lucie-Smith.

R. Lucas and James Fleet and all the staff at the University of Sussex library (where many a long night was spent researching the history of sugar cane).

Lastly, I would like to thank my family and friends, particularly my father, Alan Piercy, who has been known to appreciate a tot or two and to whom I owe my discriminating taste in the world's finest spirit.

Cheers!

ABOUT THE AUTHOR

Joseph Piercy is a freelance writer and author of over a dozen books on a range of subjects from popular history and philosophy to popular culture and the English language. His previous book for The History Press was *Slippery Tipples: A Guide to Weird and Wonderful Spirits and Liqueurs*.